Oswegatchie

A North Country River

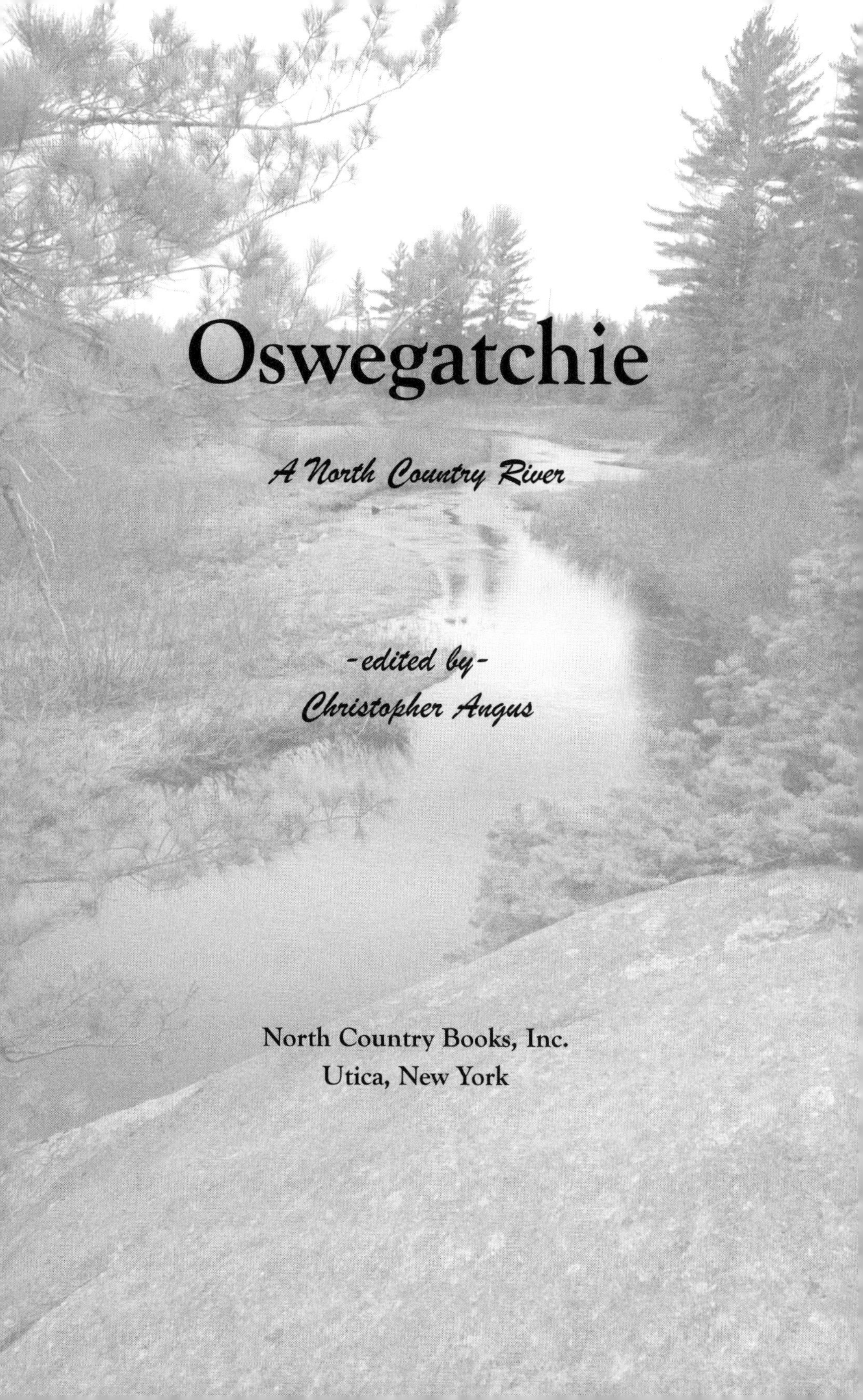

Oswegatchie

A North Country River

-edited by-

Christopher Angus

North Country Books, Inc.
Utica, New York

Oswegatchie

A North Country River

Cover Photo by Mark Bowie
Illustrations by John Mahaffy
Design by Zach Steffen & Rob Igoe Jr.

Hardcover ISBN 1-59531-007-X
Paperback ISBN 1-59531-008-8

Library of Congress Cataloging-in-Publication Data

Oswegatchie : a north country river / edited by Christopher Angus.
p. cm.
ISBN 1-59531-007-X (alk. paper) -- ISBN 1-59531-008-8 (alk. paper)
1. Oswegatchie River (N.Y.)--History. 2. Oswegatchie River (N.Y.)--Description and travel. 3. Oswegatchie River Region (N.Y.)--Biography. 4. River life--New York (State)--Oswegatchie River. I. Angus, Christopher.
F127.O9066O78 2006
974.7'56--dc22

2006013010

A version of "Early Times in the Oswegatchie Highlands" first appeared as "An Oswegatchie Odyssey" in the April 1999 issue of *Adirondack Life* magazine.

North Country Books, Inc.
311 Turner Street
Utica, New York 13501
ncbooks@adelphia.net
www.northcountrybooks.com

To my most constant advisors on rivers and writing
Jim Smith and Jamie Miller

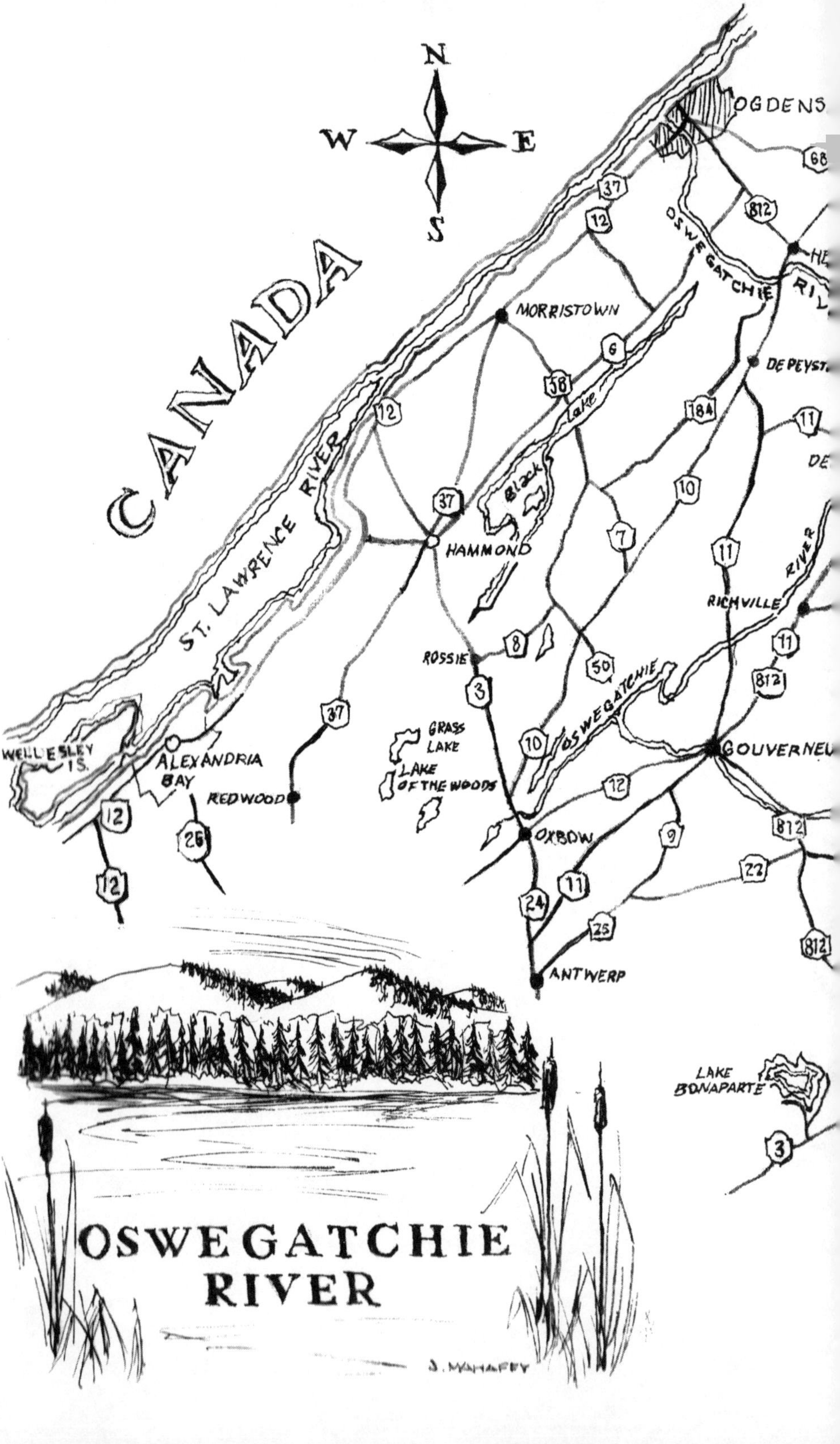
N
S
W
E
CANADA
ST. LAWRENCE RIVER
OGDENS
MORRISTOWN
DE PEYST
Black Lake
HAMMOND
RICHVILLE
RIVER
ROSSIE
OSWEGATCHIE
OSWEGATCHIE RIV
GRASS LAKE
LAKE OF THE WOODS
WELLESLEY IS.
ALEXANDRIA BAY
REDWOOD
GOUVERNEU
OXBOW
ANTWERP
LAKE BONAPARTE
OSWEGATCHIE
RIVER
J. MAHAFFY

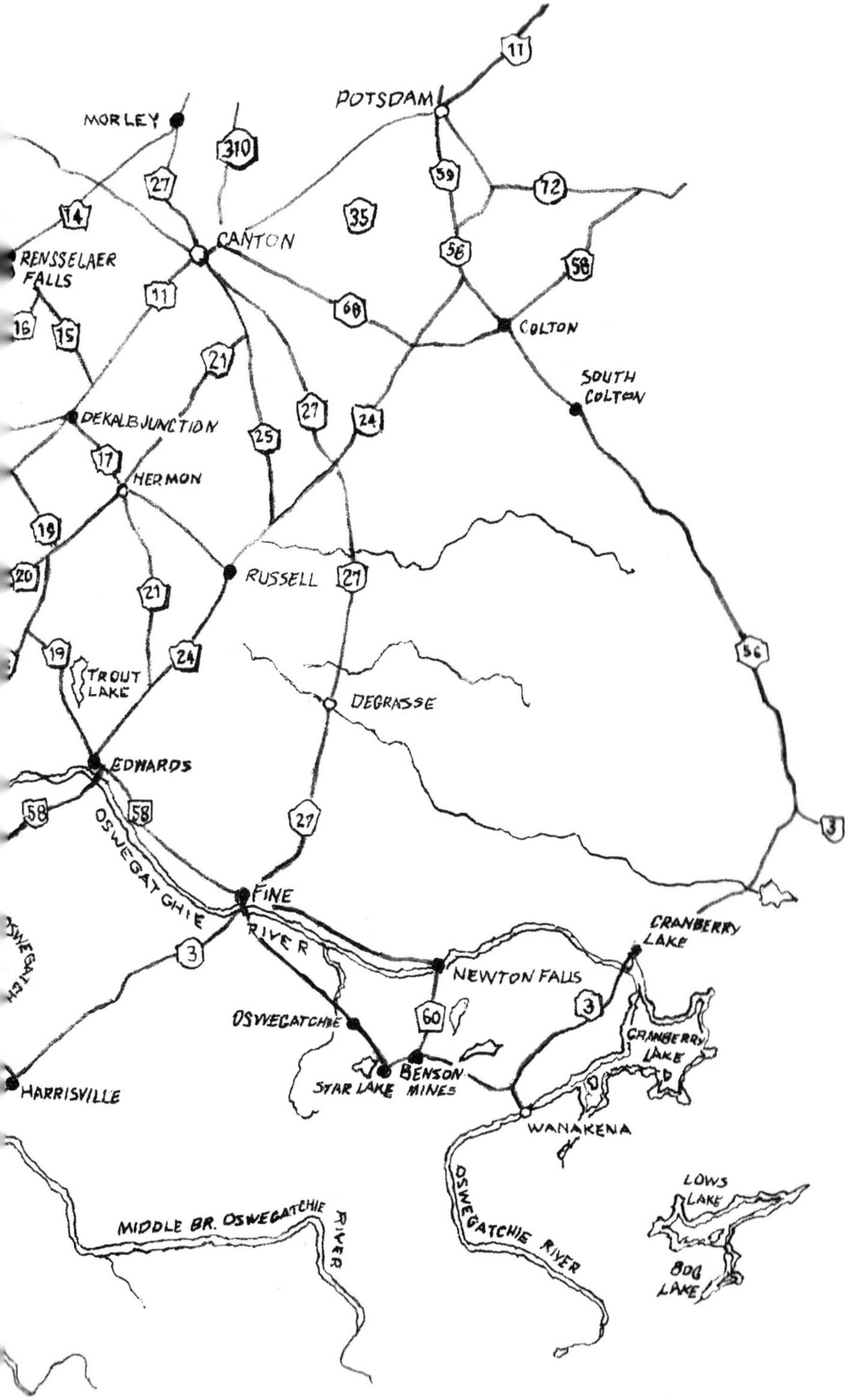

POTSDAM
MORLEY
CANTON
RENSSELAER FALLS
COLTON
SOUTH COLTON
DEKALB JUNCTION
HERMON
RUSSELL
TROUT LAKE
DEGRASSE
EDWARDS
OSWEGATCHIE RIVER
FINE
NEWTON FALLS
CRANBERRY LAKE
OSWEGATCHIE
STAR LAKE
BENSON MINES
HARRISVILLE
WANAKENA
CRANBERRY LAKE
LOWS LAKE
BOG LAKE
MIDDLE BR. OSWEGATCHIE RIVER
OSWEGATCHIE RIVER
11
310
27
14
59
72
35
56
58
68
16
15
21
25
24
17
19
20
3
60

Some men crave islands, some crave mountaintops;
It is water that calls to me.

—Robert Gibbings

Contents

Acknowledgements

Many people, including all of the contributors to this volume, have enhanced my understanding of the Oswegatchie River and its environs through their writings, conversations, and shared outings. I would like to particularly thank the following, some of whom have since passed away: Paul Jamieson, Clarence Petty, Neal Burdick, Barbara McMartin, Peter V. O'Shea Jr., Richard Beamish, John Green, Bob Patterson, Peter Van de Water, and Anne LaBastille.

There are several books I would recommend to readers interested in further expanding their knowledge of the region encompassed by this work. They are Herbert Keith's *Man of the Woods*; Barbara McMartin's *The Great Forest of the Adirondacks*; Peter V. O'Shea Jr.'s *The Great South Woods*; Albert Fowler's *Cranberry Lake From Wilderness to Adirondack Park*; and Paul Jamieson's poetic guidebook, *Adirondack Canoe Waters: North Flow*.

I owe much to family, to my parents Douglas and Sylvia Angus, whose influence grows with each year that they are gone, and to my sister Jamie, who has been editor and back-thumper at least since I was five years old. And as always, my love and gratitude to my wife Kathy and daughter Emma are beyond measure.

If not for the companionship and backwoods competence of my brother-in-law, Jim Smith, I would never have come close to understanding the many facets of the Oswegatchie River. Together, we have shared rainy nights, tipovers, aching shoulders, wildlife encounters, endless bushwhacks, and assorted injuries over more than thirty years of paddling. With luck, we may have thirty more, an unlikely achievement that would push us into that rarified realm inhabited by Clarence Petty and Paul Jamieson.

Introduction

The great wilderness writer, teacher, and guide, Sigurd Olson, once wrote: "There are certain moments when one sees more clearly, the world stands out more distinctly, and one's vision is unclouded and crystalline."

For those who climb the Adirondack High Peaks, there is no question when this moment comes. It comes at the top. It comes with the world spread at their feet, mist-shrouded or bathed in the golden haze of summer. It comes upon emerging into the high open place after hours in deep spruce woods. It comes with an intensity that, once experienced, often leads to the fierce desire to go again and again and feel the stainless steel of mountain wind.

These are the moments that create 46ers.

I can understand this, even though I will never be a member of that club. I understand, for I experience the same moments but from a different perspective. As a confirmed lowlander and lover of rivers, my view is the reverse, mirror image of the High Peaks' climbers. As they look below, I gaze on high. Their moments come while staring down at the rivers and lakes I love. My moments of vision, "unclouded and crystalline," appear as I look up at the mountains they revere. Are we different? I think not.

From the silent, snaking ribbon of the Oswegatchie River, deep in the Five Ponds Wilderness, I raise my eyes to the rims of my world, the high-crowned white pines that parade along the ridges. The hills beyond are vague, hovering forms. Many miles of hard and soft woods separate us. I imagine the climbers now fording those distant slopes. Occasionally, through the veil of leaves and needles, they may climb an outcrop and catch a glimpse of my shimmering watercourse. The view they seek at the mountain top will be vast and encompassing, but it does not alter. One view only are they allotted for their hours of labor.

My horizons change with the flick of the paddle, the meander of the stream, the slightest turn of my head. That large white pine that leans across the river ahead grows in size even as I float, effortlessly, with the current. As I approach, I detect ever more detail, the way needles seem to grow only on the top sides of branches, how thick-grained bark takes on greater definition, the certainty with which exposed roots grip hard granite. Nearer still, I hear the thrum of the pileated woodpecker's beak, the chit-chit-chit of an indignant gray squirrel, and the jazz riff of wind passing through soft green boughs.

Backdrops alter as well, frame by meandering frame, testimony to the infinite variety of this topography of wetlands, eskers, glacial ponds, and huge erratic boulders. Along one distant, verdant slope, a high line of tangled white pine, that only moments before reached out against blue sky, suddenly disappears. In its place, looming up before me, is High Rock, a twenty-five-foot-high outcropping. From its summit, I am rewarded with a panoramic view of the winding river. It is agreeable to sit here and imagine a connection with the Native Americans who surely used this site for centuries to spot game or to keep a wary eye out for enemies.

Farther along, the massive root ball of an unearthed pine snarls passage. The river is filled with obstructions this spring, just two years after the microburst windstorm of July 1995. The great roots of the toppled pine have attracted the efforts of a labor-saving family of beavers. I step onto their stripped alder branches and haul the canoe to the next level as cold water rises over my boots.

Like most of the north-flowing rivers of the Adirondacks, the Oswegatchie begins its journey in whitetail forests and ends in Holstein farmlands. It rises deep in spruce woods first ventured into by Native Americans and a handful of Jesuit priests, and spills, finally, into the St. Lawrence River. Here, where the present-day city of Ogdensburg now stands, Father François Picquet founded a settlement in 1749 for Christian converts among the Iroquois. It was called Fort La Presentation. In between those spruce woods and that great confluence lie 135 miles of navigable waters, tall pine eskers, black flies, bogs, mosquitoes, down-at-the-heels villages, coyotes, the rare moose and wolf, power boats, riverside camps, and kids rope-diving into deep black pools.

The river rises in the absolute silence of the great north woods and empties beneath concrete bridges shaking with the roar of trucks. Few see the river in its wilderness setting. Many more give only a passing glance as they cross those bridges on foot or by car, failing, really, to see it at all. Mason Smith tells of a childhood along the lower river in Gouverneur and Harrisville in which the waterway seemed innocuous, remote, something foul that the town turned its back upon. Yet it fully insinuated itself into the lives of his family and friends and was remembered fondly half a century later.

The Oswegatchie journeys from pre-history to *The End of Nature*, as writer Bill McKibben has described man's overwhelming impact on his surroundings; from springs once clean enough to drink from (no longer) to a river serving as conduit for commerce and agricultural runoff; from the rich hunting grounds of the Oneida and Mohawk to the shuttered and grim Norpac Meat Company on Lake Street.

Beauty is skin deep in this hard country, consisting of a thin crust of Adirondack soil. The soil lies like a mantle on ancient rock that bares its own history of folds and uplifts and millennia of wear. The history of the rock dwarfs the history of the soil. But it is the soil that gave us the land—gave life itself, somehow—creating us from that solid granite. It is that thin layer, the living things upon it and the waters that sustain it, that has for so long inspired men to high achievement and to deep reflection.

The great naturalist John Burroughs once stated that he was never able to separate the concepts of nature and God. Thus, he was unable to believe in an independent deity. Yet surely worship of the land is enough, for if there is an understanding God, it is hard to imagine Him not tolerating such thoughts.

The West and Middle Branches of the Oswegatchie are not as well known to the public as the East or Main stem due to steep drops and fierce posting. Access has been improving, however, and the committed paddler will reap considerable rewards if he is not intimidated. On the West Branch, spring azaleas and pink lady's slipper border chain ponds and narrow stream corridors. The upper Middle Branch is rarely visited by anyone other than members of private game clubs, though limited access is permitted. Donald Morris lauds the upper Middle Branch for its eight-mile scenic staircase in pink granite, featuring nine waterfalls and gorges with eighty-foot walls alternating with quiet pools. During May and June, he writes with co-author Paul Jamieson in *Adirondack Canoe Waters: North Flow*, "Sapsuckers hammer out a rhythmic territorial code on metal no-trespassing signs."

All three branches of the river trace their watery beginnings to the wet and wild lands of the Adirondack northwest, the Five Ponds and Pepperbox Wilderness Areas. But it is the remote East Branch and its twenty-five miles or so of easily canoeable waters, designated wild river by the state, that is best known to backcountry devotees. This section of stream boasts a rich history, yet has managed to retain a primordial quality unsurpassed in the lower forty-eight states. It is here, in the Oswegatchie highlands, that one finds the river's true heart and soul.

This is time travel, really. Paddling these sinuous waterways, one can almost see the old guides who once plied the river, Cornelius Carter, Wilfred Morrison, and Herbert Keith, as they entertain their swells while keeping an eye out for game or the perfect campsite. One can almost hear the raucous singing and hard paddling of a boatload of voyageurs. One can almost imagine a fully-laden Iroquois canoe, weighted down with a hundred beaver skins. It is here on the East Branch of the Oswegatchie, in all its protected glory, that one can today view the river almost as those Indians and early guides first encountered it.

Imagine a serpentine stream on a hot August afternoon, a dense haze like pulverized chalk hanging over everything, the high whine of a cicada piercing the heat at regular intervals, the water tea-colored, limp, languid, almost viscous, like oil flowing heavily to a distant sea.

The surface is alive with insects: water-striders, dragonflies, beetles, mosquitoes, flying ants. Few birds venture forth in the midday heat, but a single, white-throated sparrow and a pair of red-winged blackbirds pick at the smorgasbord of bugs spread before them. From time to time, a water-strider disappears in a flash of shining scale and fin as though plucked from the surface by a Grim Reaper stretching up his bony hand.

The river mirrors puffy, billowing clouds in oily reflections that ripple suddenly in the canoe's wake as though animated by a chance bluster of wind. It is an illusion quickly put to right, as the image smoothes and hardens once again on this breathless afternoon.

A paddler drifts lazily in the current, paddle dangling, its course-correcting movements barely detectable in the crook of an elbow. A pair of mating dragonflies, oblivious, land on his knee, and he resists the urge to brush them away. They quiver slightly...in the throes of something. After a moment, they fly on, still connected. It is an amazing feat of aerodynamics, as improbable as the thought of hippos mating under water. He stares into the depths. Nope. No hippos here.

Edward Abbey called the canyon country of the Colorado Plateau "a landscape that has to be seen to be believed." But this river landscape must literally be absorbed if one is to believe in it, its perfume of cedar inhaled, its haunting cry of loon and screech owl pulsed down one's spine, its taste of nitrogen savored on the tongue, as spatters of rain presage thunder clouds on the horizon. All of these things, and more, nakedly reveal what the earth is truly about...or for. In that revelation, if anywhere, man must find his own purpose, a purpose that may well be simply to witness.

In these pages, you will hear from well-known Adirondack figures who have paddled, tramped, surveyed, guided, painted, or written their way across this wilderness. You will read about the trappers, pioneers, guides, loggers, railroad men, missionaries, sportsmen, and conservationists who at various times exploited the land for its game, forests, minerals, souls, and inspiration.

In turn, it is hoped the reader will be inspired to visit, leaving behind nothing but footprints or ripples and taking away mere images and thoughts. For it will only be through widespread awareness of the special qualities of this place that we may hope to protect it from the ravages of those in every age who see value only in terms of personal gain.

Thoreau says in *Walking* that an area twenty miles in diameter will be enough to fill a lifetime of close exploration on foot; you will never exhaust the details. I would expand this sentiment to include exploration by canoe, for having spent a fair portion of half a lifetime exploring the Oswegatchie basin, I am only beginning to know the details.

—Christopher Angus

Sketches of the Human History of the Oswegatchie

Hallie E. Bond

There are many stretches of the Oswegatchie River where humans seem only incidental. Modern paddlers easily imagine themselves observing nature, not being a part of it. In this mood, it may seem strange to consider the history of the river, for history is usually understood to mean the story of humans. And while the story of people on the Oswegatchie is somewhat incidental to that of the river, especially in the upper reaches, that story provides an interesting perspective on the story of people and waterways across the Adirondacks. The Oswegatchie, like many other major rivers in the region, chiefly figured in human history by providing power and aiding—or hindering—navigation. What follows is a series of glimpses at the human history of the Oswegatchie from the perspective of a traveler. The story begins more than three-and-a-half centuries ago.

In early October of 1653, a French Jesuit priest named Joseph Antoine Poncet became the first person to travel on the Oswegatchie and write about it. His account of the trip is one of the earliest recorded first-hand descriptions of the interior of the mountains. It is brief but vivid—anyone who has been in the Adirondacks in October can conjure up a real sense of the journey from it—and it is almost as eloquent in what it omits as in what it says.

Poncet, a missionary priest, had been captured near Three Rivers on the St. Lawrence River by a party of Mohawk warriors. They took him south up the River of the Iroquois (the Richelieu), through Lake Champlain, and then west to the main villages of the Mohawk in the valley that bears their name. There Poncet was forced to run the gauntlet, was beaten and tortured, and had his left index finger cut off. Then a political situation favorable to Poncet developed, and the Mohawks decided he was worth more as a bargaining chip with the French than dead or as a slave in their villages. They put together a party to escort Poncet back to Montreal, but apparently for reasons of safety and secrecy opted not to take the easier, more direct Champlain-Richelieu route. Instead, they took what Poncet described as the other route, "taken by their armies and warriors when they came to seek us," through the interior of the Adirondacks.

For the first seven or eight days after leaving the Mohawk villages (located somewhere between Fort Plain and Indian Castle), Poncet and his escort walked north. Poncet recalled, "the rains, and the mountains and valleys; the mountain-streams and brooks, and four rivers of considerable size which we had to cross by fording, wetting ourselves thereby up to the waist; another larger one, that had to be crossed on rafts, insecure and badly put together; very short rations...all these things, I say, formed a cross for me that was so formidable and unceasing that it seems to me a perpetual miracle that I was able to bear it..."

At the end of a week, Poncet and his party reached a river upon which they traveled the last two days of the journey to the St. Lawrence. Poncet has almost nothing to say about this part of the trip, which was down the Oswegatchie. It is a shame for latter day canoeists and historians that he didn't, but this is further evidence of the difficulties of the trip overland. Two days on the river passed without comment because of their relative ease. This in itself is fairly interesting, considering the boats in which Poncet almost certainly traveled.

Poncet's escort must have made canoes on the spot when they reached the headwaters of the Oswegatchie. While these may have been dugout canoes, it is far more likely that they were bark canoes, not birch bark, which most people associate with the Indians of the northeast, but spruce bark. The Mohawk, like other nations of the Iroquois confederacy, did not make large vessels of birch bark because the area which they occupied was not good canoe-birch country. It was the Algonquin, farther north, who were the masters of the birch bark canoes. The Mohawk used birch bark canoes when they could get them in warfare or by trading, but when forced to build canoes themselves in their usual territory, they had to settle for elm or, in the higher elevations such as the upper Oswegatchie, spruce.

Spruce bark canoes had a poor reputation when compared with canoes crafted from birch, primarily because spruce cannot be formed to the fine shape that the more pliable birch bark can. Two centuries after Poncet's trip, another traveler through the Adirondacks in a spruce bark canoe wrote that he kept his chew of tobacco precisely in the middle of his mouth in order to maintain the balance of his canoe. "So long as we remained seated on the bottom, it was steady enough, but when, from our cramped position, it became necessary to change our posture, it required the skill of a rope dancer to preserve our equilibrium, and prevent one's self from being plumped into the cold waters of the lake." Still, it was better than the Indian trail up West Canada Creek.

Poncet reported no settlement or other notable features located at the mouth of the Oswegatchie on the St. Lawrence River, and it was almost a century before the area once more appeared in the written record.

When it did, it was again from the pen of a French priest. In 1749, Father François Picquet, who had already been in the New World some time and had experience among the Indians, established a settlement at the mouth of the Oswegatchie River. It was intended to serve both as a mission station and as a military outpost from which the French could keep an eye on the English. Picquet chose an admirable spot for the undertaking; Fort La Presentation was situated on a peninsula just below the first set of rapids where the river was narrow and, as one early historian put it, "the English, French, and Upper Canada savages could not pass elsewhere than under the cannon of Fort Presentation [sic] when coming down from the south." The bay formed by the peninsula was about thirty-five acres in extent, fifteen to twenty-one feet deep, rarely froze, and could be sailed into or out of with ease almost all of the time. The fort was also close to good timber reserves for shipbuilding.

Father Picquet led a fairly uneventful life at the mouth of the Oswegatchie for eleven years, baptizing the natives, teaching them to farm, helping them build houses, and generally trying to "civilize" them. He endeavored to keep alcohol from them, but this proved difficult after the garrison was manned by French soldiers. In the summer of 1751, with five Indians, he circumnavigated Lake Ontario in one "King's canoe" (perhaps a bateau) and a bark canoe. His stated aim was spreading the word among the Indians about the good life awaiting them under his aegis at Fort La Presentation, but he did some reconnaissance too—and, no doubt, enjoyed the vacation from labors at the fort.

In the spring of 1760, Father Picquet abandoned his fort at the mouth of the Oswegatchie. Quebec had fallen the previous September, and with it, French dominion over upper Canada. Picquet returned to France via the Mississippi and New Orleans. Traveling through French territory kept him out of the hands of the English, but also must have been a great adventure.

In addition to being a good location for gathering "savages" together in an attempt to teach them European ways, the mouth of the Oswegatchie had been selected by Father Picquet as being a natural trading post for trappers harvesting the furs of the interior. Very little exists in the historical record to tell us of the lives and work of the trappers who used the Oswegatchie as their highway, but latter-day canoeists can recreate their experience while traveling on sections of the upper river, since those early trappers were no doubt paddling bark canoes.

In 1803, the land around the lower Oswegatchie was being settled by groups of European-descended people, and the region provides a few footnotes to American literary history through which we get a new view of navigation on and near the river. In that year the region was visited by both William Cooper, father of James Fenimore Cooper, and the young Washington Irving. Both found the river much more of an impediment to transportation than an aid.

William Cooper, land speculator and patriarchal founder of Cooperstown on Otsego Lake, had, in early 1803, paid one dollar per acre for the 62,800 acres of DeKalb Township. In May he led a party of forty men north from Cooperstown to the wilds of St. Lawrence County to establish a settlement. Their road lay through the Black River valley and Lowville, along which, with the help of several men on either side of his two-wheeled carriage, Judge Cooper could travel in comfort. The road got steadily worse north of Lowville, however. When they reached the great oxbow in the river, they resorted to water transportation—at least for the cargo. One member of the party, Jehiel Dimick, constructed two log canoes, which he lashed together into what must have been the first catamaran seen in St. Lawrence County, and took most of the freight the rest of the way by water. When Cooper reached a spot on the Oswegatchie just downstream from present-day DeKalb village, he found a waterfall which promised industry. As he had done farther south, he memorialized himself when he laid out a town near the falls and named it Williamstown.

Washington Irving also had a nasty time traveling overland through northern St. Lawrence County. In August of 1803, as Cooper was laying out house lots and encouraging his settlers to burn the forest for potash they could sell to pay for the farms they bought from him, the twenty-year-old Irving set out from New York City to visit those investments with a party that included two investors in St. Lawrence County lands. Their destination was the village then known as Oswegatchie, formerly Fort La Presentation, and later to be Ogdensburg. They, too, traveled overland up the Black River valley and found the Oswegatchie an impediment more than a help. The road crossed the river at Heuvelton, but there was no bridge. "This would have been a troublesome business," wrote Irving, "had not Judge Ford of Oswegatchie received notice of our coming and sent men to make a raft and assist us in crossing." The fact that there was no established ferry at this crossing suggests that the traffic along the road was pretty light.

Irving found Oswegatchie itself "Delightful. After riding through thick woods for several days, with the eye confined to a narrow space and the mind fatigued with a continual repetition of similar objects, the sight of a beautiful and extensive tract of country is inconceivably enlivening. Close beside the bank on which we rode, the Oswegatchie wound along about twenty feet below us. After running for some distance it entered into the St. Lawrence forming a long point of land on which stood a few houses called the Garrison which had formerly been a fortified place built by the French to keep the Indians in awe."

Although optimistic farmers and speculators like William Cooper gradually pushed structures of civilization like forges and farms farther up the Oswegatchie, the trappers who had traveled all the way to the headwaters had left no written record of what they saw. Despite the lack of information about the upper river, or perhaps because of it, several entrepreneurs had grand visions of how the Oswegatchie could figure in the great drama of civilizing northern New York State. One Isaac Weld traveled down the St. Lawrence in 1796 and optimistically repeated, in print, the stories he'd heard that indicated the Oswegatchie rose in a pond very near the headwaters of the Hudson. Weld had also heard that both the Hudson and the Oswegatchie were navigable by "light bateaux" to their respective sources. Weld grandly proposed that the Oswegatchie-Hudson corridor become a major trade route linking the St. Lawrence settlements and the cities of the lower Hudson.

Nobody acted on Weld's scheme.

The Oswegatchie Navigation Company, incorporated in 1831, proposed a more modest plan in terms of territory, but one that came to the same end. As did other speculators and promoters caught up in the excitement of canal building during the first half of the nineteenth century, the company's officers proposed to construct locks, canals, and dams which would allow vessels considerably larger than Weld's "light bateaux" to haul agricultural products and the products from the iron forges located in the area between Black Lake and Canton. The route would go by way of Gouverneur and the "natural canal," the Upper and Lower Lakes and Indian Creek, now a state wildlife management area, which link the Oswegatchie near Rensselaer Falls and the Grass just downstream from Canton.

In his journal of the 1803 trip to Oswegatchie, Washington Irving noted that he observed the departure of "several rafts to Montreal." These were groups of sawlogs that had been tied together for transport to Montreal where they would be sold and sawn. One of the advantages of settling in the region was the many natural resources that could be harvested in the course of preparing the land for farming, and timber was chief among these. The river and its tributaries were essential in getting the logs to market. Typically, in these early years of logging, local farmers cut logs in the fall and early winter, after the crops were in and before the snow got too deep. These logs were skidded in ones, twos, and threes to centrally-located skidways where they were piled. After the first of the year the loggers packed down roads connecting the skidways, iced them, and hauled the logs out on sleds to the riverbank. At the height of the spring runoff, the logs were sent downstream individually to Ogdensburg where they were gathered together in rafts. By mid-century the logs were being collected at mills along the Oswegatchie itself and processed domestically.

So important were the rivers to the lumber industry that the state legislature began designating stretches of particular rivers as public highways shortly after the beginning of the century. In 1816, the Oswegatchie was declared a public highway to Streeter's Mills near Rossie; in 1854, the designation was extended to Cranberry Lake. This meant that the river could not be obstructed or access restricted. While the legislators of the early nineteenth century were thinking of commercial use, particularly logging, their "public highway" designation has been used in the late twentieth century as well, to argue for recreational access to Adirondack rivers.

Not that nineteenth century people were ignorant of the recreational potential of the upper Oswegatchie. About the same time entrepreneurs began taking the lumber of the upper Oswegatchie, sportsmen began taking its fish and game. In 1852, one of these early sportsmen, who wrote under the name of "Bowles" in the sporting periodical, *Spirit of the Times*, published an account of a trip he took to Cranberry Lake. Like Poncet, Bowles and his companions used a boat on the Oswegatchie, but unlike the Jesuit, they brought theirs in, rather than making it on the spot. It seems to have been a rowing boat, perhaps a St. Lawrence River skiff, and they hauled it by wheeled cart from Ogdensburg to the nearest settlement, on which journey it "suffered something by the heat and racking..." It had probably opened up and split a bit by being twisted. The worst was yet to come, at least for the sportsmen; the next seven miles were by oxcart. They arrived at the Oswegatchie and rowed or paddled up to Cranberry Lake in good form, where they spent a memorable nine days camped on the shore. The sporting was all they had wished—they took eighteen deer but made no attempt to take more trout than they could eat. Their boat floated them back to the rendezvous with the oxcart, and thence they "whirled along over fifty miles of road, rough and smooth, to the mouth of the river whose source had been to us the scene of glorious pastime..."

But more common among the sportsmen were canoes, the same type of boat used three centuries before by Poncet's captors. These were not bark canoes, by and large, but plank-on-frame canoes that were also products of the European heritage of small craft construction.

Frederic Remington, a Canton native best known for his Western art, loved the Cranberry Lake region and vacationed there frequently between 1889 and 1899. In 1892, he hired Has Rasbeck, a Cranberry Lake guide, to accompany him in his canoe, *Necoochee*, on a cruise down the Oswegatchie starting at the outlet of Cranberry Lake.

Remington was squarely in the contemporary tradition of canoeing for pleasure. The sporting periodicals and bookshelves of the day were full of accounts of canoe cruises—trips taken purely for the pleasure of paddling. In the late twentieth century, this type of recreation is taken for granted, but one hundred years ago it was looked upon with skepticism by many, including the sportsmen and their guides like Has Rasbeck. Remington wrote that Rasbeck, "being a professional guide and hunter, had mostly come in contact with people"—or "sports," as he called them—"who had no sooner entered the woods than they were overcome with a desire to slay. No fatigue or exertion was too great when the grand purpose was to kill the deer and despoil the trout streams, but to go wandering aimlessly down a stream which by general consent was impracticable for boats, and then out into the clearings where the mountain-spring was left behind, and where logs and mill-dams and agriculturists took the place of the deer and the trout, was a scheme which never quite got straightened out in his mind. With many misgivings and a very clear impression that I was mentally deranged, Has allowed that 'we're all aboard.'"

Although Rasbeck was a hired guide, he seems to have participated in the trip much as he would have if the cruise had been undertaken by two "sports." Remington's illustrations of the cruise often show Rasbeck doing the paddling and Remington enjoying the trip, but Remington does mention in the beginning that he was paddling with a double-bladed paddle. Rasbeck would have used a single blade, traditional for canoeing in the Adirondacks. The double-blade had been introduced by the contemporary fashion of cruising in decked canoes which had been modeled after kayaks and which used the kayak type of paddle.

Remington's cruise had an exciting and satisfying mix of rapid water and stillwater paddling. On stillwater, the painter's eye was powerfully impressed by the contrast between his civilized craft and "the forest primeval." The quietness of the woods, with all their solemnity, permitting no bright or overdressed plant to obtrude itself, is rudely shocked by the garish painted thing as the yellow polished *Necoochee* glides among them. The water-rat dives with a tremendous splash as he sees the big monster glide by his sedge home... The crane takes off from his grassy 'set back' in a deliberate manner, as though embarking on a tour to Japan, a thing not to be hurriedly done. The mink eyes you from his sunken log, and, grinning in his most savage little manner, leaps away. These have all been disturbed in their wild homes as they were about to lunch off the handiest trout, and no doubt they hate us in their liveliest manner; but the poor trout under the boat compensate us with their thanks."

Remington and Rasbeck's canoe cruise ended at Emeryville just above Gouverneur, in part because the river was plugged for miles ahead with logs, the results of the spring drive.

Necoochee was a "sixteen-foot canoe of the Rice Lake pattern." Rice Lake is in the Peterborough area of Ontario to the northeast of Toronto. When white settlers began moving into the area in the early nineteenth century, they used the dugout canoes of the natives as models (sometimes literally) but used their own construction techniques. By Remington's time, the term "Peterborough" or "Rice Laker" generally meant a slim, elegant craft with closely-spaced, steam-bent ribs supporting planking of narrow strips of cedar. The Peterborough area, like the Adirondacks, had become a favorite vacation spot, and the local canoes were made and sold by a number of different builders. So popular were they that the Canadian-style canoes were copied by several canoe builders in the United States. One of these was J. H. Rushton of Canton. Rushton was the best-known canoe builder of his day, a canny businessman, and a boyhood friend of Remington. He built canoes of several different Canadian models in the 1890s, and it may be that *Necoochee* was actually a Rushton.

Another Peterborough or Peterborough-style canoe is well-documented on Cranberry Lake not long after; it was paddled by Wilfred Morrison, a French-Canadian guide, and immortalized in Herbert Keith's *Man of the Woods.* Morrison paddled a Peterborough canoe in his guiding work, and apparently so did other Wanakena and Cranberry Lake guides. The Peterboroughs were fine canoes, fairly lightweight and swift. "Sports" with experience in other parts of the Adirondacks may have been surprised to see the Peterboroughs used by guides, however, because in other areas a rowing boat, the Adirondack guideboat, was the chief guide's boat. A canoe is preferred by many on a winding river, however, and it does work better if the "sport" is expected to help with the propulsion. (A "sport" in a guideboat generally sits in the stern, while the guide does all the rowing from the bow.) Wilfred Morrison sometimes poled his Peterborough, a technique often employed by guides in Maine, where the guide's boat was a canoe and where the rivers are often shallow and bottomed with small stones. In poling, the guide stands in the stern and pushes the boat forward with an iron-shod pole about ten or twelve feet long. Poling is seldom seen in guideboats, partly because of the depth of the waters in which they are frequently rowed.

Wood-canvas canoes took over the largest share of the canoe market by the turn of the nineteenth century, and it is interesting that Morrison and his colleagues didn't use them. They were cheaper than the Peterboroughs, but, some felt, not as beautiful as the all-wood craft.

If he was unaffected by the general switch from all-wood to wood-canvas canoes, Wilfred Morrison was very aware of another major change in small craft use, the application of motors. In 1908, one of the mechanics in Wanakena masterminded construction of a flat-bottomed, tunnel-sterned boat with a single-cylinder Truscott marine engine, which he used to get up to the good spring holes above Cranberry Lake. "The Beast," as Morrison called it (and which it was subsequently named), "was the forerunner of the most destructive device ever invented by man to ruin fishing on the upper Oswegatchie and other rivers." "The Beast" did not have a long career on the river—it wasn't very maneuverable—but it was indeed the ancestor of legions of power boats. Its successors were the more reliable, lighter, and cheaper outboard motors. Small ones were even used on canoes, the very boats that had opened up the river to travel by humans.

Wilfred Morrison deplored the use of motorboats primarily because they allowed more fishermen to get to the good holes than the holes could stand, but conservation was probably not his only reason for objecting to powered craft. He appreciated the whole experience of fishing and being in the woods, and of not being too obtrusive while doing it. Students of human history appreciate this too, for one of the great joys of river travel in the Adirondacks is the possibility of imagining what the experience was like in the ages before one's own. The astute natural historian can tell you that a given forest is not primeval, that it bears obvious signs of having been changed by humans; but to the average traveler, many parts of the Adirondacks, and the upper Oswegatchie in particular, seem to look untouched. Few of us are willing or able to paddle a spruce bark canoe down the river, but even in a Kevlar canoe, without the drone of that "destructive device," one can see the river as generations of Mohawks must have seen it, long before even Poncet rode it back to civilization.

The Elysian Field of Dreams

Donald Morris

In his *Seventh Annual Report of the Topographical Survey of the Adirondack Region of New York*, Verplanck Colvin wrote: "Few fully understand what the Adirondack wilderness really is. It's a mystery even to those who have crossed and recrossed it by boats along its avenues...and on foot through its vast and silent recesses, by following the long line of blazed or axe-marked trees which the daring searcher...had chopped in order that he may find his way again in that deep and desolate forest."

Among the areas explored by Colvin were the basins of the upper East and Middle Branches of the Oswegatchie. His exploits motivated subsequent generations to try to understand the Adirondack wilderness on their own terms, and they fueled my personal desire to explore these wild places.

My introduction to the Oswegatchie was probably different from that of most, who usually first sample it between Inlet and High Falls. As a budding guidebook author, I wanted to explore one of the most remote sections of river in the Adirondacks, the upper Middle Branch. State acquisitions made access to this stretch much easier than the route described in the June 1987 issue of *Adirondac*: "paddle up the East Branch from Inlet to High Falls, carry over the Five Ponds Trail to Sand Lake (more than seven miles), paddle the lake and its outlet into the Middle Branch near its head of navigability, and continue 14 miles to takeout at a woods road leading in three miles, to Streeter Lake."

In 1986, New York State's purchase of Watson's East Triangle, the largest single purchase by the state up to the 1998 purchase of Champion International lands, opened access via Watson's main haul road. In 1989, the state purchased an easement from the Lassiter Company allowing public canoeing for several miles above Bryants Bridge, the highest public crossing on the Middle Branch. These acquisitions made possible one of the most remote river trips in the state. Only the Cold River, flowing from the central High Peaks, rivals its seclusion.

I paddled the complete length of the upper Middle Branch only once, in June 1989, with my friend Chip Jenkins. I wrote Paul Jamieson to tell him our dual impressions: that this was an outstanding river and that the difficulty of the trip was such that it was probably a "once-in-a-decade" paddle. True to form, almost ten years later, some friends and I attempted to return to the headwater section. But this time, the access road had deteriorated due to damage from heavy rains following the 1998 ice storm. My resolve was only hardened, however, to return sometime soon.

In subsequent years, I often thought about that trip and how it helped define my personal concept of an outstanding river. Foremost, it should have sculpted gorges with impressive waterfalls. Make the river small, with an intimate feel, and wild, with few if any signs of encroachment by humans. Add an extended marshland, an interesting morsel or two of history to ponder, and there you have it.

Chip and I arrived following several days of heavy rainfall. After a short paddle, we entered Alder Bed Flow, as nice a wetland as I have encountered. Entranced by the flow, we drifted slowly past the alders, caught glimpses of Alder Bed Mountain through the heavy mist, and marveled at the teeming wildlife. We half expected to see a moose family come bounding down to the water's edge. But none appeared, despite what seemed a perfect paradise for them. We reflected at length about the flow and agreed that it possessed as wild and primeval an atmosphere as any we had experienced in the Adirondacks.

Soon our peaceful contemplation ended as we entered a long stretch of rapids ending near the boundary between Herkimer and St. Lawrence Counties. Here we passed close to Colvin's Great Corner monument, marking the northwest corner of the Totten and Crossfield Purchase. The easiest access by river is from the southern terminus of a trail, sometimes known as the Totten-Crossfield Trail, at a ford across the Middle Branch. But we didn't recognize the ford, and even if we had, would not have had time to explore it. Ever since, a visit to Colvin's famous marker has nagged at my thoughts. The most I've managed so far is an exploratory foray beginning at Streeter Lake.

The area from Streeter Lake southward to the county line is part of the old Schuler estate. Schuler built his fortune with potato chips. Historian Barbara McMartin relates that the tract was used to raise experimental seed potatoes far from the voracious appetite of the Colorado potato beetle. My exploration led past the fields used by Schuler, the site of his old lodge, and the mausoleum where his remains are kept. The mausoleum is the centerpiece of a small park, with perfectly manicured flower gardens and benches where one may sit and look out over handsome Streeter Lake. Just beyond is Crystal Lake, used by the family as a swimming beach, complete with white sand imported from the Niagara region. An old woods road continues south, past a beautiful loop in the Middle Branch, toward the Great Corner.

Archibald Campbell surveyed the western edge of the Totten and Crossfield Purchase in 1772, and then continued east toward Coney Mountain, near Tupper Lake, to mark the northern boundary. In 1878, Colvin left from the Beaver River region to retrace Campbell's western line, eventually crossing the Middle Branch at

Alder Bed Flow shortly before locating and marking the Great Corner.

All rivers of the western Adirondacks take their tumble off the plateau. Most, including the Moose, Beaver, Black, Raquette, and lower East Branch of the Oswegatchie, are marred by numerous dams and impoundments. The Middle and West Branches of the Oswegatchie, along with the branches of the Grass, have luckily escaped this fate and thus offer outstanding rewards. The Middle Branch's plunge off the escarpment is concentrated in an eight-mile section above and below Bryants Road Bridge. Paul Jamieson notes that a nineteenth century guidebook writer called this area the "Elysian Fields of the sportsman." No argument here.

This section is more accessible than the upper stretch, and I have visited it many times. I'm a waterfall lover, no two ways about it. Being here reminds me of the exchange in the movie, "A Field of Dreams," between Kevin Costner and his ghostly father, who has returned to play baseball in a field surrounded by corn. They debate whether they are in a cornfield in Iowa or in Heaven. An analogous question might well be pondered in the chasms of the Middle Branch.

The Elysian portion of the Middle Branch is sculpted in pink granite gneiss. The river teases with short, mild stretches, interrupted by narrow ravines and gorges, many of which are at sharp bends where the river flows around bedrock hills. This is nature at its most creative, with numerous cascades and falls, breathtaking by anyone's measure.

There is an unnamed falls near the end of this section. I call it Big Pink, though it deserves a better name. Here, you can walk out onto the pink granite bedrock at the top of the falls and step over a wide vein of beautiful marble. A few paces more, and you stand at the brink of a vertical thirty-five-foot plunge. One day I looked out through the mist into the wooded valley below and watched a deer swim across the pool at the base of the falls. I got my answer to the "Field of Dreams" question.

Two of the falls have real names. Rainbow Falls drops an awe-inspiring eighty feet into a rugged gorge. Below Big Pink is Elbow, or Sluice Falls, where the river channel is so narrow you might straddle it if you dared. I have heard that someone died here years ago, swept over the abrupt horizon line. It takes little imagination to see how this could happen.

The carries around these named falls are more difficult than they used to be since the microburst of 1995, which hit the Oswegatchie basin hard (a portion of the shuttle route is over a new road called, appropriately enough, "Microburst Boulevard"). From the ridge tops above the gorges, the full impact of the storm is evident, with downed trees scattered everywhere. But at river level, one is shielded from much of the damage, though deadfalls can still pose problems. On one trip, we found the narrow beginning of a steep ravine totally blocked by pine trees piled five and six deep. This forced us to carry around the depression where, years earlier, Chip and I savored an abundance of pink lady slippers. The tree blockage here was so bad that we thought it unlikely we would ever again be able to paddle this particular canyon. Yet on our very next trip, we were surprised to see that the trees had flushed away, a testament to the cleansing power of floodwaters.

Standing next to the cascades and falls gives one an eerie feeling, and I am always amazed at the subtlety and artistry of the river's power. In recent years, my paddling partners and I have taken to kayaking most of these falls. While this may sound crazy, it is in fact an incredible way to experience them. No doubt an artist can stare at waterfalls and years later conjure an image of them. We who run them can do the same, not so much from any imaginative abilities (at least in my case), but rather from the careful study of the channels, the rocks and ledges, and the dynamics of the water. Such study adds to the appreciation of waterfalls and can result in a correct reading that is essential to a safe and fun run. And it enables me, like the artist, to just close my eyes whenever I want and see them again.

Our runs of the drops have been largely uneventful, though occasionally someone flips and must be pulled from the water, but no one has been hurt—shaken, perhaps, but not stirred.

Chip reminds me that our initial trip, at very high water, was a bit more eventful. I had paddled way too close to the brink of a large cascade. He recalls the frantic look on my face as I strove fervently to get to shore. Funny, but it seems I had forgotten this. Chip also reminds me that I had broken my paddle at the base of one drop, requiring some quick repairs in order to finish our trip. This was one creek I did not want to be up without a paddle.

In later years, I have taken to exploring other branches of the Oswegatchie. While the East Branch is known mostly for its long flatwater cruise above Inlet, the section between Fine and South Edwards also has a number of beautiful ravines and large waterfalls every bit the equal of those on the Middle Branch. It is not nearly as wild or remote, however, and there are several large hydro dams near the bottom of the run.

In 1994, I was a participant in a "feasibility study" conducted by Niagara Mohawk Power Corporation and the American Whitewater Affiliation to assess the suitability for whitewater paddling of a section of the East Branch known as the Browns Falls bypass. This was an amazing exercise that attracted many top-level whitewater paddlers to attempt the short, mile-long section with an incredible 280 feet of gradient.

The group scouted each drop collectively, and then individual members decided whether to paddle or carry. Almost everyone carried one particularly large and dangerous falls. But three intrepid paddlers chose to run the sharply twisting thirty-five-foot drop. I'll never forget the look of total concentration in their eyes as they prepared for the run. One by one, they came down, ricocheting off a cliff wall, turning sharply, and aiming for a huge rooster tail which launched them into the air. They landed against a ledge protruding into the channel, rode the reactionary wave at the ledge's base, and ricocheted off another cliff wall before turning sharply again. Now they paddled hard to power through the huge hydraulic at the base. They disappeared under the hydraulic, but their speed carried them back to the surface downstream. This was the most impressive run I have ever witnessed. These three were on the cutting edge of the whitewater elite. A few years later, the paddling community was shaken when one of them met his death on a river out west.

One day in 1997, the Middle Branch was low, so my companion and I decided to try the West Branch from Long Pond Road to Jerden Falls. The trip begins at the edge of the Adirondack Park, not far from farming country. We didn't know what to expect, for we had never heard of anyone paddling this section of river. True to form, the Oswegatchie fulfilled our hopes. There were falls and gorges aplenty, along with outstanding scenery. At day's end, we wondered why Jerden Falls, near the takeout and smaller than most of the other falls, had obtained a name while the others remained anonymous. We wondered, too, why this section was not included within the park. To us, the river was a hybrid of the Middle Branch and the South Branch of the Grass, a pretty nice compliment. With the exception of the put-in and a small settlement downstream, it was both wild and scenic.

I continue to paddle the branches of the Oswegatchie and to explore the surrounding wild lands. For in spite of my numerous paddling trips along its watery avenues, the river remains a mystery, one I seem destined to forever strive to understand.

Riding Out the Microburst of '95

Dick and Barbara Tiel

There is hardly a breath of wind, and it's hot in the tent, even with the flaps open. We've spent the better part of this hottest of July days paddling around before deciding on remote state campsite #42 on the Oswegatchie River. We are close to where the river joins Dead Creek Flow on the southwestern edge of Cranberry Lake. After dragging sailboat, raft, and equipment to the site, we rendezvous with friends, Mike and Kathy Crowe. Camp 42 is not far from the Ranger School and provides both privacy and comparatively easy access.

We position our tent facing up the river for the view and hope for a cooling wind. The Crowes are camped on a knoll on the other side of the point near one of the larger white pines on the peninsula. Most of the night seems to be spent just trying to get comfortable or asleep. We are still awake at five A.M. and watch a light show taking place in the sky over the Oswegatchie in the direction of the Ranger School. Is it heat lightning? Just as Barbara points out that she can see rain coming down the river, it hits us.

We scramble to zip the tent. For what seems an eternity, Mother Nature flaps us about like two fleas in a pillowcase, our equipment alternately flattening upon us then tossing us skyward until we fear we may fly away. Later reports suggest that the most powerful blow lasted only three to five minutes. This is the first storm we've weathered in this tent, and we wonder what sort of defective equipment we've purchased. In fact, we later discover, our tent has actually been designed for high winds and performs rather well given the extreme conditions.

After the fierce wind and lingering rain pass, we reconnect with Mike and Kathy. They too have endured a hair-raising experience. While Mike spent his energies calculating the best escape strategy, envisioning the embarrassing conditions rescuers might find them in, Kathy practiced the soothing grounding exercises she'd learned at a workshop earlier in the week.

Reunited, we gape in wonder at the storm's aftermath. Like a sudden tornado, it has left a trail of devastation while inexplicably leaving some targets unscathed. One of our canoes has blown away, yet the other remains tied and afloat, our food still securely stashed inside. Our Sunfish sailboat is also safe on the leeward shore with raised sail, incredibly, undisturbed.

Soon, survivors begin to paddle or motor past, telling stories of incredible near misses and vast destruction. Some barely managed to escape their tents before tree limbs crushed or tore them to shreds. Others had stayed put while forest giants crashed all around them. Wide swatches of forest have been mowed down as though by a giant Grim Reaper.

We finally break camp and head back up the Oswegatchie to our vehicles. Barbara's sunning raft, the butt of jokes on the way in, turns out to be vital in bearing us and all our gear safely back to the landing. We are quite the ragtag crew, cold, tired, minus one boat, and still tense, taking in all the destruction as we paddle homeward into a tricky headwind with rumblings of more bad weather on the horizon.

Selected Poems

Maurice Kenny

Roundabout

dark, black waters
rising in the mountains
under spruce and hawk
we ripple with paddles
we break with a finger
trailing the water
we reel out a fish,
a brown or a rainbow,
we continue on
to slice the smooth face
we pause at a pool
strain for our reflection
and catch the spring
elderberry blossom

hanging out, over
the river which
eventually
will wander
through Cranberry
under the walk bridge
of Wanakena where
school girls giggle
and adolescent boys
chatter to defy the
wilderness gods and
the water gods
dare navigate
High Falls dam
as only a boy would do
not content to fish
bird-watch, berry-pick
or swim in a summer pool
of this Oswegatchie,
this black water
this ancient path
which teased Native men
to ply their dug-outs
across thousands
and thousands of
morning suns
in the good spirit
of the Adirondack mystery.

Maurice Kenny

Oswegatchie

river
    waters
in bends and turns
rapids
        and floating boughs
smooth, level face
        much of its flow
beaver, raccoon, deer
Indian pipe, trillium
        of spring
bluejays, chickadees
icy teeth
            along winter
the meandering way
from head to feet
light
    always
from head
    to feet

this river is measured
in breath,
    dark beauty
its spirit
not in inches and miles
as a map might say

Blackberrying Along the River

With dark mouth
and purple hands
the child emerged
from brambles
a tin can full
of berries
held up to
her mother
so she could see
her pickings.
Arms and legs
torn and bleeding
from her victory
harvest.

Cardinal

(March 1998 Blizzard)

red wing
        on snow
        pecking seeds
        a bluejay carelessly
        discarded
        as winds blew
        and the snow blustered
        chaotically
        yet, the hungry
bird
        such a sight of beauty
        for winter eyes
it
        pecked and pecked
        the refuse seeds
        not knowing when
        spring would ever come
                                again

(For Elaine LaMattina)

Late Summer in the Adirondacks

they have come
they have come in numbers
they have come for my
wild and red berries
they have come for my
ripe rich raspberries
the bluejays
have come

Cranberry Loons

Loons
in the black
of night
laking
Cranberry
in Kathleen's
vision
as her hand
fingers
the dark
cool
of the waters.

Berries in the Fields and on the Bush

the very common strawberry
which is no relation to the dewberry
nor the bunch berry...
the last two I would not eat
were I you.

cranberry
bogs in August with loons;
elderberry
if you can beat the birds
for the fruit, the fermented
juices;
red chokecherry
which Kathleen claims
she ate as a girl
in Star Lake;
male berry...
be careful approaching this one.

reach high for
the bush blueberry
and don't forget the bush
cranberry...
tart to the tongue...
don't make a face.

and last but not least
on my list
is
the red flowering
raspberry
(see if we can get Brett
to make a pie).

oh! golly
I forgot the blackberry
(king of them all)
the gooseberry,
current and blackcap
and there are those
who claim the beef
tomato.
(No! That is just a fruit.)

Wild Columbine

Maurice Kenny

are you the clown or the puppet
peeking through my raspberry canes?

Sitwell-pink and Emma-yellow,
purple as western sands at twilight
in Chad's Death Valley.

You flip gracefully in summer breeze,
your beauty protected
by the simple click of a camera
yet I noticed the summer morning
petals on the rain-sprinkled ground.

So much for beauty. So much for time.
(So much for forbidden abstractions.)
Brett will never let you die
especially the Emmma-yellow.

Maggots wiggle
in the belly of the dead
chipmunk also caught
in the raspberry canes
and no camera
to catch the breath.

Lost

Charles Brumley

Among the more insouciant creatures at large in the Adirondacks is, perhaps, an Adirondack guide with no client, loose. At the end of a busy and worrisomely detail-filled summer of guiding, in the can-be-idyllic month of September, I headed up the Bog River with my wife to make the traverse to the Oswegatchie. The carry had recently been opened, and while it was reported as long, we had only a couple of light Pete Hornbeck Lost Pond boats and small packs. We wouldn't have to double the no doubt well-marked carries for what we assumed would be a one-nighter. How hard could it be? We did the long shuttle to Inlet and put-in at the lower dam.

Near the upper dam, we bumped into guide Wayne Failing. As I remember, he had one of those client-friends you eventually accumulate, someone too dear to charge, but not dear enough not to. They were lazing perfectly, a few fatalistic fish on a stringer awaiting supper. In comparison, we must have appeared nearly hyperactive, fortified by delicatessen lunches, civilization in a sack. Well up the bog our first night, we had the world and the low horizon to ourselves; we owned it. I pronounced my usual mantra: "It doesn't get any better than this."

I'd paid but vague attention to the verbal details I'd heard here and there of the newly-opened carry. At the end of the bog, the take-out was about where it ought to be, and we marched off, right on by Deer Pond, where we should have put in to paddle across to the carry. There was nothing to mark this essential fact, the road or waterway not taken.

Soon, not lost, but "fogged," as Nessmuk would say, in the Cowhorn Pond region, I jogged a big loop to scout while my wife waited. Eventually, I realized that the unmarked moccasin-footway I'd passed must be the trail toward High Falls.

That trail was a wonderment of history: blow downs from many eras, pick-up sticks mish-mashed across tiny streams, a tangle so convoluted we couldn't paddle across the trickles or get our fifteen-pound boats across, short of throwing them over and climbing behind. In the old days, the trail might have had red markers.

My wife's three-day pack and her boat were ill-suited for carrying compatibility; soon she was in tears. And we were about to stay out for an extra night. We hiked on and then tented in the woods, stretching odds and ends of food. At dusk, I scouted the area. The Oswegatchie must be right over there, up that path—no, that path creeps away under alders, no action that way.

In the morning, I decided the nether-alder path had to go somewhere germane. Indeed it did—right to Camp Johnny, arguably the one campsite in the Adirondacks so precious and perfect that it parodies calendar pictures best. Camp Johnny, master of all it surveys above the upper Oswegatchie, was, and had been, empty. We were about three miles above High Falls, and the boats hadn't been in the river yet.

Now our worry was not a shortage of Oreos, but that the home-folks, who had been away, would be worried at our being out an extra day. At home, a phone message awaited us—the home-folks were staying away another day—we were not to worry.

Soon after this outing, the great windstorm of July 1995 hit the region. We realized we had taken a trip that wouldn't be there for anyone for some time. In our—my—blundering, we had gotten under the wire for one of those experiences that is remembered when the trips that are too perfect are forgotten, faded into a blissful and indolent haze.

Wolves Along the Oswegatchie?

Christopher Angus

Caribou have been gone from Adirondack country for thousands of years. The last native elk to be shot in the region may have been dispatched along the Raquette River in the 1840s. Most agree that the wolverine and catamount are no longer with us, though the number of diehards who swear they have encountered the Adirondack cougar is increasing. Still present in the early years of the new millennium are bobcat, peregrine falcon, and perhaps even lynx, though it is the nature of these creatures to have a thin population spread over a large area. The bald eagle and wild turkey, benefiting from human intervention, are doing well. Beaver and bear, hunted to extremes in the early part of the century, have also made an impressive comeback. Moose, rejected in the 1990s as a species worthy of reintroduction, return at their own pace. But the wolf, once hunted as ruthlessly as any creature on this earth by the chief species extinction agent, Homo sapiens, has been unable to effect its own return. Its reliance upon man for help rests upon a dubious history.

In 1630, the Massachusetts Bay Colony offered a bounty of forty shillings—a month's salary—for every wolf killed. This was probably the earliest such bounty in the new world, initiating a hunt that would not sputter out until the wolf had been extirpated from all but the farthest northern edges of its historic range within the lower forty-eight states.

In the Adirondacks, bounties were paid on wolves, panthers, and numerous other creatures considered undesirable, including one of two cents in Lewis County for chipmunks. In the early decades of the 1800s, bounties paid for wolves dropped off sharply in all Adirondack counties with the exception of Franklin, where the combined state and county bounty was sixty dollars, a huge amount of money at the time. All the wolves left in the Adirondacks seemed to concentrate, somehow, in Franklin County, where from 1820 to 1822 hunters applied for fifty-five thousand dollars. Since this money came from taxpayers, the hoax caused something of an uproar. Finally legislators, while declaring their sympathy for the citizens of Franklin who obviously had to dwell among crazed wolf packs, decided to appropriate just one thousand dollars for wolf bounty each year. If one wolf was captured, that was the bounty, but if a thousand wolves were caught, then the bounty was one dollar each. Miraculously, wolves disappeared from Franklin County almost overnight.

Wolves have been clubbed, poisoned, burned alive, pulled limb from limb by men on horseback, clamped in steel leg traps, impaled in pit traps, shot from airplanes, crushed by deadfalls, choked in rawhide neck snares, killed for scientific experiments, and baited with spring-loaded fishhooks embedded in tallow that sprung in the gut causing internal hemorrhage. For their part wolves have, on rare occasion, killed Indians and Eskimos, destroyed loved pets, transmitted rabies, exhumed dead bodies, and eaten livestock. (I have relied on Barry Lopez's seminal study, *Of Wolves and Men*, for some of the background information in this essay.)

The disparity between the purported and actual frequency of these behaviors, however, is huge. For wolves have been nearly eradicated by man in North America, killed in untold numbers ever since that first bounty set more than 350 years ago. They have been destroyed with a vengeance and a cruelty almost beyond comprehension, the more so given man's long love affair with a close wolf relative, the domesticated dog. "If dogs were to inherit the earth," Edward Hoagland once wrote, "they would quickly turn into wolves again." Some people, writes Barry Lopez, kill wolves "habitually, with a trace of vengeance, with as little regret as a boy shooting rats at a dump."

Through much of American history, wolf hunting was considered a fine, even moral, pastime, pursued by many upstanding members of society. Theodore Roosevelt, who fought wolf predation on his ranch in North Dakota, called the wolf "the beast of waste and desolation." He once set off on a wolf hunt with seventy fox hounds, sixty-seven greyhounds, and forty-four other hunters, beaters, wranglers, and journalists in a private train of twenty-two cars.

George Armstrong Custer hunted wolves, running them down in open prairie country with his huge staghounds. Even naturalist Ernest Thompson Seton, who personalized and humanized the animals he wrote about, nevertheless devised clever means of bait poisoning that allowed him to catch a pair of famous outlaw wolves in New Mexico.

The wolf has long been the victim of misinformation and myth. "Everyone believes to some degree," Lopez writes, "that wolves howl at the moon, or weigh two hundred pounds, or travel in packs of fifty, or are driven crazy by the smell of blood. None of this is true."

What is true is that wolves as we know them have been a highly developed predator since the early Pleistocene Epoch, a million years ago, and a variety of wolf-like creatures have inhabited the earth for tens of millions of years. They have adapted to nearly every habitat available to them from the Siberian steppes and the islands of Japan to Morris Jessup, Greenland, 400 miles from the North Pole. They will eat almost anything from mice to moose, including marmot, beaver, crayfish, salmon, Dall sheep, fiddler crabs, elk, deer, caribou, ducks, geese, squirrel, domestic stock, berries, carrion, and even insects. They are opportunistic hunters, a highly developed and useful trait that preserves energy in the wild.

Wolves range in size from 45 pounds for an adult Arabian wolf to 120 pounds or more for an Alaskan wolf. The largest wolf on record is a 175 pound animal killed in Alaska in 1939. Wolf pelts range in color from cinnamon, chocolate brown, and gray, to slate, blue-black, blonde, and nearly pure white. The animals generally live in packs which are really extended families of from two or three to as many as twenty. The largest authenticated report is of a pack in Alaska of thirty-six. Wolves can run at speeds of up to thirty-five miles per hour and can clear sixteen feet in a single bound. While hunting they can maintain a pace of about twenty miles per hour for many hours, eventually wearing down even the swiftest prey. The wolf's closest relatives today are the dingo, coyote, jackal, and domestic dog.

Such facts have been hard to come by in the past. Even today, there remains much to be learned about wolf habits and biology. For the wolf has been caught between two great, contradictory images of wilderness, as evil and desolate, worthy only of conquest by man, or as a spiritual retreat, majestic and deserving of preservation. Our legends and literature are filled with this dichotomy. There is the ancient image of the benevolent wolf-mother as portrayed in the legend of Romulus and Remus and in Rudyard Kipling's "Mowgli." Contrast this with the fierce image of the wolf in "Little Red Riding Hood" and "The Three Little Pigs," not to mention the horrific pursuit and burning of men, women and even children who were accused of being "werewolves" during the Middle Ages.

It is these latter images that have made the effort to restore wolves to the American landscape so difficult. One group that has taken on this herculean task is Defenders of Wildlife, a Washington D.C. based conservation group that has led the campaign to successfully restore wolves to Yellowstone National Park. In 1995, 14 gray wolves were released in Yellowstone. The following year, 17 more were added. Today, some 130 wolves in thirteen packs, considered the maximum feasible number, inhabit the park. Buttressed by the migration of additional wolves from Canada, many more now roam the Northern Rockies.

Defenders of Wildlife has also been a force behind efforts to assess the Adirondacks and parts of Maine for similar efforts. In casting about for the best places to reintroduce wolves to their former range, the group settled on a region largely drained by the Oswegatchie River, the Five Ponds Wilderness south of Cranberry Lake.

It's a natural choice. The Five Ponds is at the core of the proposed "Oswegatchie Great Forest" that would comprise some half million acres without a major road. Such remoteness would seem to present the perfect location in which to allow the wolf its freedom. Wolves were once a part of this vast ecosystem, largely responsible for its natural balance and for the evolutionary beauty and grace of many of its species through the systematic pruning over thousands of years of the weak, old, sickly, and deformed.

Writer and longtime wilderness guide in the Quetico-Superior country, Sigurd Olson, understood this role of the wolf. More than fifty years ago, in words that have hardly lost their relevance, he wrote: "We still do not appreciate the part predators play in the balanced ecology of any natural community. We seem to prefer herds of semi-domesticated deer and elk and moose, swarms of small game with their natural alertness gone. It is as though we were interested in conserving only a meat supply and nothing of the semblance of the wild. If the great gray timber wolves ever leave the Quetico-Superior, the land will lose its character."

The return of the wolf could go a long way toward restoring the natural balance of a deer herd that is today deemed too large. Human complaints of deer browsing in flower and vegetable gardens, striking automobiles, and spreading ticks and disease would seem to reinforce calls to restore the wolf. In areas where wolves have been reintroduced, the increase in tourism has been in the millions of dollars each year. Places like Canada's Algonquin Park and Olson's Quetico-Superior trumpet the fact that the cry of the wolf can be heard round the campfire at night. This lonesome, haunting cry is probably a call to assemble the pack, pass on an alarm, or locate each other in unfamiliar territory. But many who have witnessed wolves in the wild describe an almost joyful element to the group howl.

As an "apex predator," the presence of wolves has a ripple effect on an ecosystem. Their presence in Yellowstone has changed the park's ecology in many ways. The elk population, unused to the presence of wolves since the 1920s, has declined considerably, and a renewed respect for the predator has driven them to high ground, away from browsing on willow shoots along rivers and streams. As a result, willows have returned in great profusion. For similar reasons, cottonwood and aspen have also rebounded.

More trees stabilize the banks of streams and provide shade, which lowers water temperature and improves the habitat for trout, resulting in more and larger fish. New vegetation has also led to an increase in songbirds like the Lincoln sparrow and yellow warbler. Willow and aspen provide food for beaver, increasing their numbers on the northern range, resulting in many more dams and flooded lands. Carcasses left by wolves benefit other carnivores, including scavengers like magpies and ravens. Reeling from the competition, the number of coyotes has fallen by half, allowing their prey—voles, mice and other rodents—to increase. That in turn bolsters the red fox and raptor populations.

Experts believe these profound changes will continue to grow and ripple through the ecosystem. Thirty years from today, Yellowstone will be a very different place, certainly one more in tune with its natural history prior to man's arrival. (Information on the effects of wolves in Yellowstone comes from "Hunting Habits of Yellowstone Wolves Change Ecological Balance in Park," by Jim Robbins, the *New York Times*, 18 October 2005.)

In 1998, the Adirondack Association of Towns and Villages, which represents most of the communities within the Park's boundaries, passed a resolution flatly opposing Defenders of

Wildlife's plan to reintroduce wolves into the greater Oswegatchie Basin. The State Farm Bureau added its opposition, citing a belief that wolves would increase their range to the farms in and around the Adirondack Park, threatening livestock. Several local county legislatures also weighed in with resolutions declaring that they too were against the reintroduction of wolves, against even "studying" the issue. That the St. Lawrence County Legislature was among the most vehement is hardly surprising given that the last bounty paid on a wolf in New York State occurred in St. Lawrence County in 1899.

There appears to be a sort of natural panic attack among some when this issue is raised, against all reason and evidence. For in fact, there has never been a recorded death or even attack of a white man by wolves, although there have been many such by a wolf relative, the domesticated dog. Even when wolves were more common, there was little to be afraid of. In his 1869 classic, *Adventures in the Wilderness*, William H. H. Murray wrote: "They are only too anxious to keep out of your sight and hearing. Touch a match to an old stump, and in two hours there will not be a wolf within ten miles of you."

Wolf populations have always been easily controlled due to the creature's highly developed social structure which places a ceiling on its population growth. By way of contrast, scientists have estimated that 75 percent of a given coyote population would have to be killed every year for fifty years to bring the population to extinction.

In Minnesota, where there is a large wolf population of about 2,500, the livestock depredation rate has been less than one-half of one percent (and there are programs in place to reimburse ranchers for the occasional loss). Retired biology professor and noted canid expert Dr. John Green of St. Lawrence University says that, "The fear instilled in us by legends and myths is unwarranted...fear of attack by wolves is unjustified." Still, legislators called plans to reintroduce wolves "stupid" and their own opposition a "no-brainer," a declaration certain to be viewed in more ways than one.

Small populations of wolves have established themselves in Wisconsin, Michigan, Montana, Idaho, and Washington. Their numbers have increased naturally in the Superior National Forest of Minnesota, and they have been successfully reintroduced in New Mexico. In 1987, the red wolf was restored in eastern North Carolina. "For a while," writes Bill McKibben, "the red wolf had not existed; it was alive in a zoo somewhere, but that was nothing more than keeping its DNA on ice."

Calls for wolf reintroduction have occurred in many other states. In addition to providing a complete ecosystem, the presence of wolves has been shown to drastically reduce the numbers of coyotes, which are in no danger of extinction and which have been getting bad press of their own lately following the near abduction of several children. As seen in the Yellowstone example, fewer coyotes leads to an increase in other small mammals, rabbit, fox, woodchucks, and field mice, thus providing increased food supplies for fisher, osprey, eagles, and other desirable predators. Moose, deer, and beaver are the wolf's major prey. Landowners who have lost woodlands and seen roads flooded from beaver activity should welcome the wolf.

Perhaps the greatest problem the wolf faces is that it has no natural human constituency, unlike that not so endangered species, the county legislator. Wolves don't pander, and they don't act irrationally. Rather, they are creatures of logic and high intelligence. Lobo's reward for such admirable behavior has been eradication from more than ninety percent of its former range.

In a 1998 hearing on the matter before the St. Lawrence County Legislature, among the few voices raised in support of the wolf were those of a group of high school students and their biology teacher. The young people were not afraid of wolves. That fear seemed to rest firmly in the hearts of the more senior lawmakers, who were unwilling even to await the results of studies before declaring their opposition, even though it was by no means certain that such studies would have supported wolf restoration.

Shortly before this meeting, I received a call from Steve Kendrot, who was leading the fight for Defenders of Wildlife. He asked if I would make a statement on behalf of wolves. I had always believed, almost intuitively, that the return of the top predator would be a good thing, completing the circle of life and bringing balance to the ecology of the region. Even more basically, says writer Bill McKibben, "Restoring animals means restoring the spirit of a place." But after considering the matter, I realized that I had very little knowledge of the issue and declined to speak from a baseline of ignorance. Kendrot's query spurred me, however, to begin the research for this essay.

To my surprise, I found a considerable degree of ambiguity. It is uncertain if repopulating the wild with animals bred in captivity can be achieved. Defenders of Wildlife's successful reintroduction of wolves to Yellowstone was achieved through the relocation of wild wolves, which appears to be a more successful method. Yet even this must rely on extremely careful efforts to avoid lengthy separation of animals from their habitat to prevent behavior distortions. A program to reintroduce the Mexican wolf, a subspecies of gray wolf, in Arizona's Apache National Forest, met severe losses from hunters. Bred in captivity, the Mexican wolves quickly learned how to hunt, but they didn't learn how to run away from people. In their pens, they moved 100 feet away and then stopped. In the wild, they did the same thing. Unfortunately, this behavior didn't take them beyond the range of a gun. This is no small issue. The state of Wyoming still has a law from frontier days that classifies wolves as predators and lets them be shot on sight.

Captive breeding programs are expensive. Plans to restore the condor, black-footed ferret, and wolf have already cost more than $50 million collectively. Such programs have been seen as doing little to address problems like poaching, habitat loss, fragmentation, and pollution that are pushing species toward extinction. Perhaps the money could be more effectively used in these efforts. Other difficulties arise from a lack of space and resources for preserving species indefinitely, the development of behavioral problems, and inbreeding that can lead to genetic abnormalities. In 1994, Dr. Benjamin Beck, associate director of the National Zoological Park in Washington, found that out of 145 documented reintroductions in this century encompassing 115 species, only sixteen produced self-sustaining populations in the wild without human assistance.

But this story is not simply one of success rates and cost-benefit analyses. Kristen DeBoer, director of the environmental group RESTORE: The North Woods, writes: "Wolf recovery is not just about restoring the wolf. It is about beginning to reweave the whole fabric of life. It is about biodiversity and wilderness restoration. It is about how we define our role in nature. It is about our worldviews. It is about lifestyles. It is about values. What good is wolf recovery if we do not simultaneously work to restore the ecological integrity of the North Woods?"

I can imagine few things more satisfying than sitting under the stars listening to the howl of a wolf. I have been suitably thrilled to hear the yelping of a distant pack of coyotes. How much greater my sense of place in the cosmos if I were able to hear the cries of a wolf pack reverberating across the Adirondack hills?

Yet still I hesitate. I fear that when conservationists declare the return of the wolf to be a bell-weather issue, they play into the hands of those who stand ever ready to declare environmentalists nothing but a bunch of sentimental "bunny-lovers." The wolf is a hot-button issue, one viewed irrationally by many Americans steeped in that long history of myth and misinformation. Perhaps we need to pick and choose our battles with more care. By taking a line-in-the-sand stance on the return of wolves, we may hurt our credibility and consequently our chances to promote other, more urgent, environmental needs.

Maybe this is a cop-out, a way to avoid a terribly difficult and contentious issue. But politics, to borrow a worn phrase, is the art of compromise. The *New York Times* weighed in on this very issue in an editorial (8/14/98): "One of the hardest problems facing anyone who cares about environmental matters is keeping a sense of scale. The big battles are so wearing that it can be hard to concentrate on the small ones...But the principles that govern the environmental movement are not scalable."

In the best of all worlds, principle should always be the most important thing. But when one has dealt for a while with the harsh reality of day-to-day politics, he begins to learn the necessity of compromise and, yes, of "scaling" the importance of various issues. After the presidential election of 2000, the United States lurched from the potential of having a committed environmental president in Al Gore to electing the most anti-environmental leader imaginable, the oil and mining industry's great good friend, George W. Bush. Environmentalists have had to make many hard choices in the years since then.

As a somewhat timid public spokesperson, I admit to admiring people with strong beliefs who are unafraid to speak their minds. Edward Abbey had something to say about this that should strike close to the hearts of all writers: "I've done most of my defending of the West with a typewriter, which is an easy and cowardly way to go about it. I most respect those who are activists...There are thousands of people involved in conservation, thousands, and they should all be named, if it were possible—the people who actually carry on the fight, who do the difficult work of organizing public resistance, who do the lobbying and the litigating, the buttonholing of Congressmen, or in some cases, who run for public office, who draw petitions and circulate them, who do the tedious office work and paperwork that have to be done to save what's left of America. I respect those people very much. I respect them much more than people who merely sit behind a desk and write about it."

I now believe I was wrong not to speak in favor of at least *studying* the wolf issue. For that is what was being debated at the forum. Not if the wolf should be brought back, but whether we should allow our duly elected legislators to bury their heads in the sand and declare that they would not even *consider* the results of studies before making up their minds. This was a forum for speaking out against small-mindedness. That's what that high school biology teacher and his students were doing, and they were way ahead of me in their thinking.

Perhaps we recognize our own natures in the wolf. As we have seen, wolves have a dark side along with their caring nurture of their pups, their sometimes carefree play, and the pure joy of their howling sessions. But the occasional act that we may find distasteful arises nonetheless out of instinct and the need for survival. Humans, too, have a dark side, an almost innate capacity for cruelty, well proved by our history. Yet it is more difficult for us to lay blame on instinct. Maybe it is shame at our own shortcomings that leads us to strike out in anger at the wolf.

Some years ago, Governor Walter J. Hickel, a Republican, decided that something was terribly out of whack in the wilds of Alaska, America's final wilderness frontier. There were too many wolves, he declared. Wolves eat moose, the preferred prey of that two-footed predator, the human hunter. To keep more moose alive so they could be shot by Alaska's hunters, wolves had to be killed. "We can't just let nature run wild," Governor Hickel declared.

Those words are a crystal example of that dark side, that selfish side of human nature that has been so damaging to the creatures that share this planet with us. Yet despite the still widespread acceptance of this kind of cavalier and ignorant attitude, Barry Lopez believes that "as the twentieth century comes to a close, we are coming to an understanding of animals different from the one that has guided us for the past three hundred years."

I am not quite so hopeful, for as we continue to radically alter our planet's ecology and continue to cause extinctions at an alarming rate, it seems at least possible that by the time enough of us finally reach Lopez's *understanding*, the wild creatures will be all but gone. Aldo Leopold once wrote: "Conservationists assume that a day will come when we will all want to pick up the pieces...It is a questionable assumption."

Yet nature continually surprises us. In 2002, a wolf pack was discovered in Quebec not far from the Maine border, raising the possibility that wolves will spread into New England and eventually the Adirondacks on their own. This may be their only hope, as conservation groups and governmental agencies continue their complex dance over the issue. A 1999 study sponsored by Defenders of Wildlife concluded that wolves would not be able to survive in the Adirondack Park over the long term. However, a study commissioned by the Wildlands Project in 2003 concluded that the western Adirondacks and neighboring Tug Hill Plateau could support up to 400 wolves.

The Bush administration, meanwhile, has shown increasing hostility to the Endangered Species Act, at least partly to appease land developers, farmers, and ranchers who complain about restrictions in their property rights. The government views delisting species like wolves and grizzly bears as the best way to deregulate, because the species will no longer be protected. But in two recent court cases, one filed by Defenders of Wildlife and eighteen other groups, federal judges ruled that the U.S. Fish and Wildlife Service violated the Endangered Species Act when it abandoned efforts to restore gray wolves throughout much of its historical range, including the Northeast. It is uncertain if the Fish and Wildlife Service will appeal the rulings.

The conflict and confusion seem destined to remain for the foreseeable future. Yet undeniably there has been progress with regard to how at least some people perceive the wolf. Not everyone wants to kill them at first sight—though few of us ever have the opportunity to see wolves today. And despite the many problems associated with reintroduction, it remains a hopeful sign that there are groups actually working to protect wolves, working to open the door at least a crack for them in remote places like the Oswegatchie Highlands.

Tripping the Wet Fantastic

Christine Jerome

Our Oswegatchie paddle in early October 1991 was to be a reunion. John and I had been separated for several weeks as I wrestled with a manuscript at an artist's colony in the central Adirondacks. The plan was for him to come over from Massachusetts with gear and food for a two-day expedition. I remember pacing the porch, scanning the driveway and wondering what was taking him so long. It was raining but the air felt balmy. Better it should rain now and clear in the morning, I thought. Finally my consort wheeled into sight, and I flew to the car, duffle bag whacking my legs. We'd reserved a motel room in Long Lake (first things first) and planned an early start next morning.

The drive to Inlet the next day was made under somber skies. I remember being amused at the town marker that read "Fine" just before we turned off Route 3; what would come next, "Dandy?" We'd opted for a midweek put-in in hopes of securing a lean-to or choice campsite, but the congested parking lot seemed as unpromising as the skies.

No sooner had we finished packing our eighteen-foot Wenonah than the heavens opened. Throwing a tarp over the load, we raced back to the car and threw ourselves inside just as thunder boomed overhead. "Welcome to the Oswegatchie; Have a Nice Day." The downpour lasted ten minutes before subsiding to a moderate sprinkle. Anxious to get under way, we sponged out bow and stern and then shoved off, rain pattering on our hoods. Happily, the air remained relatively warm. We'd gone less than a mile when another deluge descended, this time with sheets of water so dense we sheltered, hanging onto boughs, under a spruce. I was getting grumpy.

Now we entered the swamp, where the river's sinuous course demanded bow steering, a skill I'd never needed before. Our previous river runs had all been made in small solo canoes; the Wenonah Jensen, designed to track like an arrow across large water, proved to have the turning radius of the QE2. After a couple of ignominious encounters with riverbanks, John showed me how to angle my paddle at the bow, and our progress became less fraught.

High Rock would have made a fine lunch site, but two canoes were already there, so we pushed on through intermittent showers. A couple of campsites on the right bank were strewn with large hunks of junk, no doubt relics of the old days of motorized access. On we paddled, disappointed beyond measure to find the lean-tos near Griffin Rapids and Buck Brook occupied, their residents glumly staring at us through a scrim of rain. Why didn't they go home? I wondered. Nobody seemed to be having much fun.

At a grassy flat on the left bank, we disembarked for a late lunch sandwiched between showers. It was here that John discovered he'd forgotten the cheese and salami that were to have been our fare, but we made do with peanut butter and fruit, and our spirits brightened as our stomachs filled. The swamp was behind us, and the river was now the woodsy thoroughfare we like best.

The rapids we encountered were too shallow for paddling, and since we had no poling experience, we lined the canoe through them, slipping on rocks and getting soaked to the waist. It's hard to be cheerful, I find, when your underpants are wet. Our energy was fading along with the light, and a low-grade panic began to seep into my psyche. Where would we stay? When would the cold descend? Would it ever stop raining? Around each bend I hoped to find a campsite—I was no longer holding out for a good spot, only a habitable one—but nothing presented itself.

We had ascended the river about ten miles when another shower and failing light forced us to accept the next space that opened up. Just beyond a great gouge in the left bank where a tree had been pried out, we scrambled ashore at a sloping clearing with space for a tent and a tarp, no more. It was as minimal a spot as I'd ever contemplated camping on, but the prospect of getting back into the canoe and finding nothing else for a mile reconciled me to staying there. The rain moderated to a drizzle.

John soon had a tarp rigged, under which we gratefully changed into dry clothing. As comfort returned, so did good humor. In no time the tent was up and we were home. A quick meal revived us further. So cheerful was the light cast by our Swedish stove that we kept it going long after dark, lounging beside it with wine in our mugs.

The chilly, clear dawn heralded a lovely day that had us peeling off layers as we continued upstream. In a little more than an hour we'd gained our turnaround point at High Falls. Here too the lean-tos were occupied, and several paddlers were admiring the cascade and clambering around on the rocks, as we did.

Descending the river was as much fun as we've ever had in a canoe, a rollicking, gleeful careen accomplished in what seemed like half the time of our ascent. The day was transcendent as only a perfect October day can be. We ran rapids and beaver dams, with joyful whoops erupting from bow and stern. Finding High Rock deserted, we claimed it for a leisurely lunch and watched a large buck negotiate the far side of the swamp, moving purposefully to the north. Soon we were back among the meanders, our shadows, as Paul Jamieson so aptly put it, circling around the boat. Far, far too soon we were back at put-in—weary, dirty, happy campers.

Oswegatchie Odyssey

Nina H. Webb

A job description circulating around the cavernous halls of the capitol building in Albany, New York in 1871, might have read like this: Wanted: Rugged individualist, compulsive about goals, capable of overcoming physical and emotional challenges; must have uncanny ability to recognize century-old survey markers. Applicant should be fiercely committed to this job, able to sustain high energy levels despite lack of food and comfort, and willing to compromise friendships in order to achieve goals.

Those familiar with Adirondack history will know that there was only one man who could fit such a characterization. His name was Verplanck Colvin, the man hired by New York State to survey six million acres of Adirondack wilderness during the latter part of the nineteenth century. Colvin became a legend unto himself, and as he roamed the woods from 1872 until 1900, he left lasting trails of scientific findings, numbers of accurate topographical maps, and scores of fascinating annual reports. Among his most important contributions were the efforts he made to convince the populace and the bureaucrats that the Adirondack wilderness needed to be preserved. His relentless commitment eventually gave New Yorkers Article VII, Section 7 (The Forever Wild Amendment), the

New York State Forest Preserve, and our unique Adirondack Park.

In order to handle his huge assignment, Colvin divided the Adirondacks into regions and surveyed each of them in depth. His goal was the production of one large topographical map of the entire area. During the summer of 1878, he worked in the northwest region and focused his energies on the Oswegatchie River territory. His study of ancient maps and charts revealed the existence of an important boundary marker on the northwest corner of the great Totten and Crossfield land patent, the spot at which Totten and Crossfield's holdings joined those of Alexander Macomb. At that particular juncture, many survey lines radiated into the wilderness like spokes on a huge wheel. Re-establishing that particular corner became key to Colvin's work, and he resolved to follow one of the "spokes" from Beaver River all the way to the corner. The resulting expedition turned into quite a saga.

Colvin had been in the Oswegatchie area before, once on his own before the Adirondack Survey began, and again in 1873 when he did some topographical work near Cat Mountain. While there he met John and George Muir, two locally famous guides who regaled him with stories of the Oswegatchie wilds. They told of beautiful hidden ponds, panther and wolf sightings, and of huge speckled trout leaping onto their lines. Colvin was a superb fisherman, and their stories whetted his appetite. He couldn't wait to begin his search.

The so-called Great Corner had been established by colonial surveyors in 1772, just after Totten and Crossfield had purchased approximately 800,000 acres from the Mohawk Indians, and then again by early Adirondack surveyors in 1853. By the time Colvin came around, the old lines leading toward the corner had become blurred and obscured, and there was some doubt in his mind that the true corner would still be recognizable.

But challenges were nothing new for Colvin, and he set to work organizing his assault. Gathering the proper crew to help would be critical to his success. When word of his plans reached the ears of the locals, he was overwhelmed with applications. His name had become such a drawing card that even those who lacked basic surveying and survival skills applied. Colvin chose strong, burly, young men to carry supplies and instruments and older, wiser men "who had grown gray in the surveys of the forest" as his assistants. Among them was a bearded old man who, twenty-five years earlier, had hammered a stake at the very spot Colvin aimed to find. The thought of going down in history as the one who relocated the famous corner fueled Colvin's egotistical fires. On July 8, 1878, the man author Paul Jamieson once called "a backwoods President de Gaulle," was off and running through the woods.

Following the old lines turned out to be a significant test of Colvin's observational skills. Not only had the passage of time obscured the markers, but loggers, trappers and other surveyors had put their own markings on trees and rocks. Later, when he wrote his annual report for 1878, Colvin said that he found the area a "confused chaos of dubious lines and false topography."

Even when he was able to sort out the mess of lines, Colvin had trouble recognizing overgrown markings. Many blazes were moss-covered and hidden on the trunks of downed timber. It was then that the old men he had chosen to accompany him came into their own. They were masters at recognizing signs, and they taught Colvin everything they knew. The intrepid surveyor soaked it all up. Before long, he too could identify little, green, sunken spots on the undersides of old, moss-covered trees. In fact, he became so good at it that the old-timers ended up praising him, a fact Colvin did not hesitate to mention in his reports.

The Oswegatchie country was dotted with lakes and ponds, many of them tributaries and feeders of the great river system. Every time it rained, those waterways flooded, forcing Colvin to slog through swamps and marshes and to make broad detours in order to reach his destinations. In those days, the woods were plagued by forest fires. Often, the atmosphere was so smoky that it was difficult to take readings or to sight lines. But by far the biggest challenge was the fallen timber. There were acres and acres of crisscrossed trees lying in crazy-quilt patterns, making passage almost impossible. Clawing through the slash carrying heavy packs was back-breaking work. By the end of the day, Colvin was often as exhausted as his men. One evening, he calculated that it had taken them all day to move two miles closer to their goal, while his pedometer had recorded eight and three-quarter miles of walking.

Colvin's men were dedicated and loyal. No matter how tired they were, they cheerfully constructed camps and shelters and hunted for fresh meat. They were masters of everything from cooking to chopping and could skillfully apply huge slabs of waterproof spruce bark to their shanty rooftops. Colvin was lucky to have such men on his teams, and despite what his detractors have said, he did appreciate their loyalty. One only has to read the words in his 1877 report to know the depth of his feelings: "To my faithful guides, who labored—some of them refusing all reward, long into the dark night, hewing the great fire-logs that, kindling into fierce flames, made the wild winter forest laugh with their light and heat—to those men who, tenderly wrapping me in my blanket, turned to watch the camp fire through the night, I tender my heartfelt thanks."

Colvin was fascinated by the wild country he was traversing. From previous reconnaissance he had learned that he was to cross a huge basin through which the Oswegatchie meandered like a giant snake, sucking its sustenance from hundreds of waterways as it rambled toward the mighty St. Lawrence River. He absorbed the ambiance, reveled in the lowlands, and exulted from the high spots. When the atmosphere was clear, he climbed mountains to get better views. He gleefully described finding a fallen tree on a mountain summit, positioned in such a way that he could mount it like a diving board and view the mysterious region below. He was mesmerized by the excitement of exploration and discovery, and despite the intensity of his work, was able to record, in meticulous detail, his reactions to the natural beauty he encountered. That excitement spilled right onto the pages of his annual reports to the New York State Legislature. To this day, his words captivate and thrill readers lucky enough to find original copies.

When Colvin and his crew left Beaver River on July 8, he fully expected to locate the corner within a week's time. But by the fourteenth, they were still thrashing about, and Colvin became concerned about keeping to his summer schedule. With that in mind, he ordered his men to throw aside all unnecessary baggage. They would carry only the instruments, axes, and provisions. They made another of Colvin's famous "forced marches," hoping to reach the corner by evening. But by late afternoon, Colvin was acutely aware that his men were exhausted, so he called a halt and ordered them to make camp on the shore of Wolf Lake.

Still brimming with energy himself, Colvin headed off to explore the lakeshore. He was delighted and a bit mystified to find himself on a "singular long narrow dune...open and picturesque with superb white pine trees...the beautiful Wolf Lake on one side and a shallow winding river on the other..." It seems strange that Colvin didn't recognize an esker, nor did he figure out that the "shallow river" was a lake whose waters fed directly into the Middle Branch of the Oswegatchie. Today we know those bodies of water as Rock and Sand Lakes.

When writing about that discovery, Colvin mentions that he had taken an assistant with him to explore the shoreline. But for reasons unknown, Colvin was alone when he experienced a near tragedy. It seems that he decided to circumnavigate the lake and return to camp along the northern shore. When hiking through the woods became too tough, he waded along in the shallow water. All went well until, "I entered a cold heavy quicksand, and descended so suddenly that I had barely time to grasp some laurel bushes at the shore, and with difficulty escaped entire submergence and drowning." Where was the assistant? Had he gone back for help? Was he really with Colvin, but gone unmentioned because Colvin wanted to be the hero of the escapade? Who knows? It was a close call and makes one wonder what would have become of the Adirondack Survey had Colvin perished in the sand.

By July 15, Colvin felt that they were close to the corner and that by nightfall they would be celebrating. So they pushed on. At one point, while crossing an open hardwood forest, the keen-eyed surveyor spotted some "shapely footprints" around a damp spot on the ground. It turned out to be a deposit of marly clay where deer came to pick up nutrients lacking in their everyday diets. Not only had Colvin noticed the footprints, but he had seen the little, smooth spots made by their licking tongues. He wrote that it was the only natural deer-lick he had seen in the Adirondacks.

Later, when they came to a branch of the Oswegatchie flowing through a large swamp, the Muir brothers' promise of good fishing came true. In no time at all, they had caught a "handsome string" of speckled trout to take along for supper. Having had a little fun, they pressed on, climbing up and down ridges and following the faint signs of the old survey line. At 5:00 P.M., the men called a halt. This was a highly unusual event. Colvin was the boss and the one who called the shots, but not this time. His men were utterly exhausted and refused to go on. For once, the boss had no choice. They made camp, ate their fish, and retired for the night. A frustrated Colvin estimated they were only one mile from the corner.

Rejuvenated by a good night's sleep, they left camp early on the morning of July 16. Traveling lightly without their cumbersome packs, they moved quite easily. Colvin, in his eagerness, struck out ahead. He crept through wind slash, crossed brooks and swamps, and ran along the banks of the now familiar Oswegatchie. He could smell victory, and he wanted to be there first.

Close to where his calculations had told him the corner might be, he came into a sort of glade, a level place surrounded by old, standing trees. The line he had been following was no longer visible, a clue to the fact that the corner might be near. Colvin stood quietly and studied the surrounding trees. He noticed some "singular hollows and contortions" in the bark. Then it hit him. These were the witness trees! Each was blazed on one side only, all pointing toward the center of the glade. Colvin looked down at his feet. There he saw the remains of a crumbling, wooden stake with three little moss-covered stones at its base.

He had found it! Here was the pivotal point on which land titles to millions of acres depended. He was thrilled, and when his men caught up with him, and the old surveyor confirmed Colvin's discovery, the woods resounded with their shouts of joy. It had been a tough eight days, and all were glad when it was over.

After a brief rest and a meager lunch, Colvin ordered his men to find a large boulder, suitable for a permanent marker. They searched the woods and eventually came up with a stone weighing an estimated quarter of a ton. With great difficulty, they rolled it to the site and dug a huge hole beside it. After Colvin had measured and re-measured the exact location of the corner, they levered the monster into the pit. Several drills blunted and splintered in the tough rock before the hole marking the center of the station was completed. Then, in a repetition of a routine they had followed many times before, the men melted some lead, poured it into the hole, heated the copper bolt (Colvin's signature marker), and set it into place. After gathering smaller stones and heaping them into a huge pyramid over the monument, they stood back and reflected upon the importance of their discovery. They had found and marked one of the most important boundaries in all of New York State.

Colvin's delightfully detailed sketch of this final scene appears in his Seventh Report. It is classic Colvin. Is that a self-satisfied smile on his face?

Author's note: In the Adirondack Mountain Club's *Guide to Adirondack Trails 2: Northern Region*, there is a fine map and description of the Totten and Crossfield trail which leads determined hikers to the famous corner. In 1903, New York State surveyors re-established the corner over the spot where Colvin had placed his historic monument.

A Wide Spot on the Oswegatchie

Michael Kudish

Cranberry Lake is a wide spot on the Oswegatchie River. In 1968, as a graduate student, I attended a summer session at the Barber Point Biological Field Station on the shores of this third-largest lake in the Adirondack Park. Two State University of New York centers were then jointly operating the field station, the College of Forestry (since renamed E.S.F.) at Syracuse and the University at Albany. I was a Syracuse student and had to travel to Albany to register and then obtain transportation to Cranberry Lake—a long way around, it seemed. To this day, I still wonder why I could not register and travel directly from Syracuse.

Once the crew of faculty and graduate students arrived at the hamlet of Cranberry Lake, I realized that the only way to reach Barber Point was to take a boat; there were no roads into the field station. Once we arrived, I also realized that there was no electricity into the field station from the outside world. A diesel generator provided power and a constant drone. Fortunately for me, it had frequent breakdowns, plunging the field station into much-needed peace and quiet.

On many days, the biology students would head off, bushwhacking into trail-less woods for several miles to work on their various course projects. They would be gone all day, taking their lunch with them. About midday, the students would become aware of a rustling in the shrub layer. The noise of snapping twigs and crunching leaf litter would become louder and louder as the intruder approached. Several of the students, especially urban and suburban students, showed some alarm. Could it be a bear? Their concern turned to laughter when the field station caretaker's large, friendly Saint Bernard emerged from the bushes. The dog routinely managed to follow the students by scent to their project areas, staying always a few hours behind, showing up just in time for lunch.

We once had an all-day bushwhack field trip to Wolf and Graves Mountains. After our study of the summit and a steep descent, we began to head north over the rolling, pond-dotted plain back towards the field station. The professor (no, it was NOT Ed Ketchledge) then veered off in a different direction: a side trip, we students thought. Then he took another turn, and then a third, and a fourth. We were soon wandering all over the headwaters of the Oswegatchie. Those of us students at the back of the long, single line, with compass and altimeter in hand, were following the circuitous route on the topographic map the whole time. Late in the afternoon, at the shore of a small pond, the professor finally stopped and admitted to us that he was lost. So we pulled out the map, showed him the peripatetic route that he had been leading us on for several hours, and then led him back to the field station.

River Reflections

Clarence Petty

In 1958, Assemblyman Watson Pomeroy was appointed to chair the Joint Legislative Committee on Natural Resources. I was delegated to act as DEC Liaison Officer to that committee for a Study Bill on possible wilderness area designation for Forest Preserve areas in the Adirondack and Catskill Parks. That year, Neil Stout, Executive Director of the Committee, Watson, and I canoed up the Oswegatchie and spent the night in what later became the Five Ponds Wilderness Area. During this outing, Pomeroy took photos of brook trout trying to jump High Falls.

Neil and I stayed all over the Adirondacks during our studies, and we always had to carry everything we needed. A lot of the time, everything was closed down. You couldn't find anyplace where there was a hotel or motel, and we had to bring our own groceries. Otherwise, you'd end up starving to death. We slept outside on the Oswegatchie trip and most other trips, though we occasionally got to stay in places like Paul Schaefer's little cabin when we were working up in the Bakers Mills area, outlining the region for the Siamese Ponds Wilderness.

Starting in 1971, one of my assignments with the Adirondack Park Agency was a study of Adirondack rivers in preparation for the State Legislature to designate wild, scenic, and recreational rivers. The Oswegatchie is one of the few rivers that has all three designations within the Park. Over 1,300 miles of river was studied from source to the Adirondack boundary, including details such as stillwater, rapids, wildlife habitat, vegetation, man-made structures, and so forth. This experience gave rise to my belief that streams are to the Adirondacks what the arteries and veins are to the human body.

The Oswegatchie River provides the public with one of the very few canoe access routes directly into the heart of a large wilderness area. The river was quite famous as a brook trout stream, and one day an author on the subject of trout fishing, whose last name I believe was Everett, asked me to take him fishing. He caught and released many trout and may have written about the experience in one of his articles for *Field & Stream*.

Cranberry Lake and the Oswegatchie River received considerably less fishing pressure during World War II. As a result, the fishing immediately after the war was excellent both above and downstream from High Falls. On one of my inspection trips, a fisherman at High Falls asked me to take a large trout to Wanakena for storage in a refrigerator, where I had it weighed. It was a few ounces over four pounds.

When I was a district ranger covering the county, one of my forest rangers was Fred Griffin, whose father was a settler at Oswegatchie. Fred told me that his father cut swamp grass along the river between Inlet and Griffin Rapids to feed his cow and horse. Obviously, there was little open land suitable for pasture or hay.

My father, Ellsworth Petty, was a guide around the Saranacs in the late 1800s. He got most of his "sports" from that area, so his experience with the Oswegatchie was limited. His cousin, Carlos Whitney, who also guided, chiefly from Upper Saranac Lake, did say that on a trip through the Bog River to Cranberry Lake he saw the largest white pine that he had seen in the Adirondacks. That was in the 1800s, before much of the logging occurred.

Most of the virgin pines are gone now, taken by loggers as well as natural forces like the Big Blowdown of 1950, the microburst storm of 1995, and the ice storm of 1998. I remember going hunting on the day of the 1950 storm. It was an overcast day, and the wind was just roaring like the devil. Of course, I didn't know it at the time, but it was the side of a hurricane coming up the coast. It took down a lot of trees in the Five Ponds Wilderness. It also took one pine behind our house that was fifty-four inches in diameter. I still have some of the wide boards we had cut from it in my barn.

It was the last day of hunting season. I left home at daylight and got pretty high up on Stony Creek Mountain when I saw a buck. There were trees falling and limbs coming down all around me. I had to look up all the time to keep from getting hit by something. But it was a beautiful day to hunt, because it was so noisy that you could walk right up to a deer and he couldn't hear you coming.

The next morning my brother Bill, who was the regional forester, said, "All the telephones are down, everything's blocked, and there's a survey crew stuck up along the Cold River." He was real concerned, so he headed out to start work getting that road open. I went up to the Five Ponds, because I had charge of the whole area. One of the things I had to do right away was to get the trails to the cabins and the fire tower opened up for fire control. But we got hit with snow soon after the hurricane and that knocked the fire hazard down.

I had rangers working on the lines up to Cat Mountain and Tooley Pond. I went into Five Ponds by myself to see how things were in there. I took a bow saw and a hand axe with me. As soon as I crossed the bridge at Five Ponds, I found a bunch of little tamaracks that had fallen across the trail. I started by cutting the tops off those little tamaracks with the bow saw. Pretty soon, I got hot. I was wearing my Navy flight jacket, so I took it off and laid it on one of those trees I'd cut.

Well, I worked my way into Five Ponds, and I was gone about three or four hours. After crawling around through all that downed timber, I figured it would take a crew of four about three days of work to clear out that trail. Coming back, I got almost to the bridge and I said, "God, what did I do with that jacket?" I'd laid it down on a tree and I looked all over and I couldn't find it anywhere. I went all the way back to the river—thought I must be losing my marbles. I wondered if someone had come along and taken it. Then I was looking down and noticed one of the trees I'd cut was starting to lift up—you know—spring back up again. So I looked up, and there was my jacket thirty feet in the air, stuck in that tree. I had to take my bow saw and cut it down to get my jacket back. That was a good jacket; I didn't want to lose it.

I had responsibility for checking on the guys who had gotten the bids for salvaging the downed timber. The Conservation Department had asked the state attorney general for special permission to let them remove the downed logs, which was not allowed by the Constitution. There was a bunch of bonded Canadians up there cutting on Pine Ridge. One day I found one of the lumberjacks about to cut down a good pine tree simply because a branch had been knocked off by a tree that had fallen down next to it. I said, "You can't cut that tree. That's a good tree." He spoke French, only a little English. He says, "The tree is damage, the tree is damage." Well, I said, "There's nothing in the contract that says you can cut it," and he stopped.

As it turned out, it went down later from another blowdown anyway, but that was the sort of thing that happened. I later found a huge white pine right on the Oswegatchie River that had been cut down. Of course no one would admit to cutting it. But that's what was going on; they were only interested in getting the volume of timber out, and there were a lot of violations. State foresters were supposed to be checking up on those guys, but a lot of them didn't care about what was cut or not.

I was always in a disagreement with the foresters who couldn't care less about what happened in the Adirondacks. One suggestion I made to the Division of Lands and Forests was that they work with the people in Albany who make up the competitive exams, because maybe they could have found out that way whether an individual was in favor of Article XIV (Forever Wild) or whether he was against it.

There was a lot of controversy about wilderness areas when they were first proposed. One of the things I thought we should do was find out how far these places were from a public road or waterway. A lot of the people who were against wilderness and its restrictions on motorized access were saying, "These areas are so remote that nobody but the most physically fit can get in there."

So I decided to find out just how remote they were. We spent a good deal of time during our last winter at the Study Commission, going all over with a map and finding out where the margins of the wilderness areas were and how hard it would be to reach them. We found that thirty-eight percent of them were less than a mile from a highway or public waterway, and eighty-two percent were within three miles. Most of them were right along some public access point, and you could walk a mile or two or get in a boat and be there in a few minutes.

It was amazing, really, and it didn't go over too well with the people who were saying that the wilderness areas were so remote.

The Oswegatchie Inlet

Paul Jamieson

Early and late, the Oswegatchie is a storied river. The northern boundary between two Iroquois tribes, the Mohawks and the Oneidas, it was their route in raids against the Hurons of Canada. In 1653, a Jesuit priest, Father Joseph Poncet, became the first European of record to traverse the western Adirondacks from the Mohawk Valley to the St. Lawrence, two days of that journey on the lower Oswegatchie. And in 1749, another French priest, Father Picquet, founded a settlement at the mouth of the river for Christian converts among the Iroquois.

But it was not until the twentieth century that a chronicler appeared to do for the upper Main, or East, Branch what Mark Twain had done for the mighty Mississippi. Herbert Keith's *Man of the Woods*, published in 1972, tells the story of a boy who, like Huck Finn, absorbs forest and river lore from an older mentor. In 1907, Adirondack guide Wilfred Morrison introduced twelve-year-old Herbert to the Inlet by a canoe trip upstream to Beaverdam above High Falls. Herb took fire. In this and subsequent summer vacations with his uncle in Wanakena, he resolved to make that hamlet his home for life, however risky it was to make a living there.

Like other enterprising natives, Herb became a jack-of-all-trades.

One of them was guiding parties up the Inlet to his guide's camp between Round Hill and Crooked Rapids or beyond. But the last good decade for guiding was the 1920s. Herb had to turn to other trades. When I knew him during the last decade of his life, the 1970s, he had retired except for repairing his neighbors' radios and selling copies of his book to stragglers coming out of the Five Ponds Wilderness at the corner of his lot. Canny as ever, he told me that there was no use selling his book to neighbors. One of them with a lucky windfall would buy a copy and then pass it around to all the others. Downstate sports were a better market. So he would autograph his book on the title page, pocket the trade discount from list price, and await the fan letters that were sure to come.

Herb had worked for several years on his book, perhaps in self-vindication vis-à-vis his high-powered third wife, a quarter-century younger than he. Mimi had been an art student in her native Sofia, Bulgaria. She spoke five languages. She gave art and piano lessons to the wives and kids of the Ranger School faculty in Wanakena. She made oil paintings of landscapes in nearby woods and waters. These were widely disseminated in the homes of neighbors. (A painting is not something you pass around.) I have two of her paintings, both of tumbling brooks embowered in emerging spring-green foliage.

Mimi was the final phase in Herb's development. She smoothed his rough edges. As I knew him, he was a man of natural dignity, ripeness, and solidity, who had always known how to cope. And he was full of anecdotes about life in the woods and on the river.

The Keiths lived in a long, low house Herb had built himself. His lot line bordered state land. The Five Ponds Wilderness stretched for fourteen miles south to the Stillwater of the Beaver in what is probably the most authentic wilderness of the Northeast; more than half of it had never been logged before the state acquired it. Deer browsed on Herb's lawn. Raccoons ambled in to dine with the family cat. The river was a stone's throw to the north. Herb's life was intimately bound up with it. He knew its every bend. By local count there were two hundred of them in the twenty-one miles above Cranberry Lake to the head of navigation. The locals scorn that official estimate of distance; they say it is at least thirty, probably more. All those bends! Some backwards! Where for a mere quarter mile the river straightens out, this singular eccentricity is called the "Straight of Way." The river's meanderings through boreal marsh and forest, its quickening and its slowing, exert a powerful effect on the affectations and imagination. Four centuries ago, Tasso sang of the enchantment of a river bend. Herb was not a poet, but in sentiment he came close. His book celebrates those bends by attaching stories to a good portion of them. But for him, the folklore of the Inlet might never have been recorded.

August Afternoon on the Middle Branch

Neal Burdick

"Do you think we can get through it?"

"Sure, we'll hug the left bank and you draw hard to the right just before the break in the snag."

"OK, let's go."

My friend Alex Velto and I are canoeing upriver on the Middle Branch of the Oswegatchie, a few miles above Harrisville. It's a calm stretch of river, tying together forest and farmland, and after several miles and ninety minutes of paddling against the modest current, we have not yet come upon a blockade we cannot circumvent. This one, though, looks a little more imposing than the others—a large tree, possibly brought down by the 1995 microburst, lying across almost the entire channel, with a considerable supply of branches, sticks, leaves, pine needles, and even a Styrofoam picnic cooler jammed up behind it.

Sure enough, we hang up on a submerged limb as we swing around the deadfall. No amount of rocking can free us. Finally, we admit defeat, and I clamber out of my bow seat onto the wall of rubble. With my weight gone, Alex can maneuver his sixteen and one-half foot Mad River Malecite fiberglass canoe over the trap, and we are once again free to follow the watercourse upstream, out of the St.

Lawrence valley, into the Adirondack Park and into the Great South Woods.

We had put in that morning at a bridge on Steam Mill Road, a few minutes east of Remington Corners. We'd had for an audience a crew of county highway department workers, taking shelter under the bridge as a rain shower passed through. They seemed bemused by two strangers hauling a canoe and its inevitable accessories across several yards of blowdown, slipping on the muddy bank and generally attempting to choreograph a put-in where there really wasn't room for one.

The difficulty of the put-in, confounded as it was by a jumble of tree limbs and trunks, products of both the microburst and the January 1998 ice storm, and by some most inconveniently placed rocks in the water, contrasted with the ease and pleasantness of moving on the water. It's no wonder that the native peoples who visited the region to hunt, fish, and fight regarded the waterways as thoroughfares. Slipping easily into a rhythm calculated to overcome the gentle current, we caught up on each other's children, our work—some years ago we'd been colleagues in the same division at St. Lawrence University—and the general state of the world. In that fluid environment, where the mere stroke of a paddle could move us forward without undue strain on the heart, without panting, without fear of a turned ankle; where land and its problems seemed a universe away, even though it was often no more than an arm's length; it was simple to solve every one of society's most perplexing dilemmas.

Getting past a truly mountainous and diabolical snag, though, is not so simple. It barricades the entire channel as effectively as a dam, and there is nothing for it but to go ashore and carry around the obstruction for about fifty feet. This, of course, necessitates unloading all the gear, hauling the canoe up a four-foot vertical bank, carrying it and the paddles, cushions, knapsacks full of lunch, water bottles, and raingear, etc., maybe twenty-five steps—being careful all the while to stay below the not perfectly well-defined high-water line, since PRIVATE PROPERTY signs blare from every third tree—and then reversing the whole process, except down an even higher vertical bank. Maybe there are things to be said for hiking, after all.

> The Middle Branch here travels through two forest transition zones: the "macro" zone that undulates across North America and marks the change from the northern boreal forest to southern deciduous, and the "micro" zone that indicates the shift from the uplands of the Adirondacks to the lowlands of the St. Lawrence Valley. Thus the river takes us through a virtual arboretum, a pleasing, often open, mixed forest of maples showing their first hints of fall colors, aspen, beech, birch, cherry, the ubiquitous alder, pine, hemlock, tamarack about to go to gold, and even some oak.

This is the sandiest river I've ever seen in the Adirondacks. Other rivers have an occasional patch of sandy bottom, a sandy few feet of bank, maybe a sandbar every so often. But this one is sand-lined for miles, although few if any of its sandy shore stretches would qualify as beaches. Whereas on many rivers the rocky banks are broken by a rare patch of sand, here the sand is interrupted occasionally by a rock, polished by centuries of wear and tear by the relentless black water of the Oswegatchie.

Indeed, this is the blackest water I think I've ever encountered, which is appropriate since the name "Oswegatchie" is said to be Onondaga for "black water." If that's true, this river and its other two principle branches are well named. Of course, Paul Jamieson in his classic *Guide to Adirondack Canoe Waters: North Flow* relates the story that the river's name memorializes the experience of some early New England explorers in the area, whose horse got away from them. They chased it until it came to the river, which it found too deep to cross, whereupon the explorers exclaimed, "Orse, we got cha."

I tell Alex that story. He's not buying it.

There's a transition of time as well as distance going on. Midsummer plants remain, but the late-summer ones, those that make the preliminary announcements that warm weather's days are numbered, also abound: the brilliant red cardinal flower, blue gentian, goldenrod, milkweed in its early tender green.

A couple of hours in, we pull up on the bank to explore what appears to be a man-made forest to the east. Surmounting an esker, we survey parallel rows of evenly-spaced red pines—likely a Civilian Conservation Corps reforestation project from the 1930s, making these forty-foot-tall trees roughly sixty years old. There's evidence of some harvesting, some thinning, but it's not recent; the county seems to have abandoned its commitment to good forestry practices even as its leaders condemn the state for not allowing forest management in the nearby "forever wild" Forest Preserve. Gnats attack our eyes as the midday heat, made more pronounced by too much humidity and too little breeze, grows oppressive; we retreat to the world of the river.

For a while upstream from here, the Middle Branch has so many oxbows it may as well be the Mississippi. We zigzag, for maybe a mile, in order to cover a few hundred linear yards. Map and compass skills are pointless in canoeing; one goes where the water goes and doesn't give much shrift to bushwhack short cuts.

An otter plunges into the water and swims ahead of us, bubbles every few yards marking its progress. We catch a hawk circling on thermals and a turkey vulture scanning the ground for a meal. A kingfisher darts from branch to branch. We spot bear scat on a sandbar. A heron—we can't tell if it's a great blue, and joke that maybe it's just a pretty good brown—erupts out of the water as we approach, flies gracefully ahead of us, lands and repeats the process as we draw near. It repeats this performance several times, and we wonder that it doesn't simply fly out of our path; and yet, like us in our canoe, it is wed to the water—land is an alien, dangerous environment, and to fly toward us, so as to go over our heads and thus put itself behind us, probably goes against its instincts. We hold back a little, and, rounding a bend, do not see it again. Later we spook a deer and her young, drinking at the water's edge; they bound away into a thicket of alders. Yes, I know—all writing of this sort seems to have a deer or two in it, but we really did see them. Ask Alex.

The water in this river, or at least this portion of it, doesn't seem to be in a hurry to get anywhere. But that's one of the great things about wilderness: there's no need to be in a hurry to get somewhere, because there isn't necessarily a reason to get there. Time is different in the wilderness than it is in those vast areas of the world that man has subjugated. It is measured differently (say, by the season instead of by the hour) because it operates differently. The annual progression of leaves on a maple tree is a better timepiece than a watch. Time doesn't much care what mere mortals have to say about it, and that is one reason why we should leave in peace what wilderness we have left on this planet.

And yet this river, or at least this portion of it, is not a wilderness river. Like most of us, it has its heart partly in the wilderness, partly in civilization. We disembark at a bend, the better to view what appears to be a clearing; it turns out to be a cow pasture, farm buildings and a house beyond, a road with power lines draping along it just past. Our sense of immersion in the natural world is constantly broken by the concussions of artillery practice at Fort Drum, which is only a few miles away. We bravely try to pretend that thunder is the generator of the rumbles—storms were in the morning forecast and the day has grown sticky enough—but they're too regular, too artificial, too low to the ground. We spend an inordinate amount of time oxbowing under a series of power lines, the 765-KV arteries humming as though to say, "What chance does wilderness have when our steel towers carry electricity to millions of city-bound people who don't particularly care whether or not it goes through a Forest Preserve to get to them?" In mid-afternoon, two planes, also probably the responsibility of Fort Drum, split the sound barrier and scream past, seemingly at treetop. As we near our turn-around point, camps—some in better shape than others—line the river, and another county road crosses overhead on a steel bridge.

A short way upstream from this point, we do an about-face and begin to retrace our route toward our put-in point, the current with us now. But we linger for a moment before we let that current take us back, take us downstream, down toward the St. Lawrence Valley with its farms and towns and factories and tamed land, toward our cars with their reminders of clocks and families and jobs. The lure of the true wilderness, farther upstream, around who knows how many more bends, is strong. We've heard the river gets rugged and spectacular up there, white and churning and rocky. Is that its wilderness personality, its Jekyll to the placid Hyde it presents as it nears the world of human society? Some day, we vow, we shall find out...

> In a wetland to our right, a single maple stands, its leaves bright crimson even with autumn still several weeks away. Like Moses' burning bush, it sends a message that certain forces will not be denied.

As we did coming up, at some point on our return we cross the Blue Line, the fabled boundary of the Adirondack Park. It isn't identified with a fancy wooden sign along the rivers as it is along the roads, although each is a highway after its fashion. But maybe that's just as well. Perhaps it's better not to know. The integration of wild lands and tamed, forest and field, populated and not, should be part of our thinking about how we use physical space everywhere, not just in a park. Our experience this day is not diminished when we leave the park; in fact, if one criterion for a "good" experience is perceived distance from evidence of human presence—other than our own—

we are better off where we are not in the park, or think we are not, for there is less sign of civilization. The camps we saw were inside the park; outside, we travel through unadulterated forest.

> The river supports its own circles of life, separate from, and yet strangely united with, the circles on the land and in the air. Fish occasionally dart under us; sometimes they are but shadows, and always they are too quick for us to identify them. How something as unwieldy as a bear can catch one with its bare hands is one of those mysteries of nature that will astound me as long as I live. Water-darters—at least, that's what we decide they're called—look like figure skaters practicing their routines. For every insect we can see there may be thousands we cannot; some of these will before sundown become the sustenance of the fish we've seen when they make the rare break of the boundary that separates their environment from ours. A bullfrog broadcasts a warning that sounds like a bass player lustily plucking his lowest string.

At some point on our downstream run, one of those booms in the sky actually does sound more like thunder than war games. With the next one, there's no question. In a few moments, rain begins to fall gently, pocking the river's surface and pinging against the canoe.

"Think we should get out the rain gear?" Alex asks.

"Nah. The way I sweat in that stuff, I'll be as wet with it as without it."

"Me too," Alex says.

The rain comes down harder and harder; soon the banks of the river, only a few feet away, are screened by a gauzy veil. We are in the middle of an orchestra careering through a saturating symphony.

We're thoroughly soaked by now. With a shrug we don the rain gear.

The rain doesn't last long. Like most summer thundershowers, it takes only a few minutes to pass over us, moving off to rumble and dump its moisture somewhere else. With the slow return of the sun through haze, the leaves, the river, the sky, even our paddles acquire a sparkle. Drops falling from branches glisten like so many tiny chandeliers. The shower has brought out the fresh aromas of all the living things around us. And now it matters even less where that park boundary is. It matters not at all whether planes annoyed us, whether this river is wild enough to suit us, whether we'll be home in time for dinner, what bills came in the mail. The moment is to be savored. And that is why we came, and why we will return.

Early Times in the Oswegatchie Highlands

Christopher Angus

River corridors like the Oswegatchie have long been at the center of human forays into the Adirondacks. More than five thousand years ago, the Late Archaic peoples moved into the drainage corridors of these mountains. They are identified by their spear points which were smaller than those of their predecessors, the Paleo-Indian hunters, who left projectile points along the shores of the inland sea, now Lake Champlain, eleven thousand years ago. This decrease in weapon size corresponds with the extinction, around 8000 B.C., of the caribou, bison, and mammoth.

The Archaic culture of St. Lawrence County is called the Laurentian culture. The Laurentians hunted bear, deer, and elk, fished the streams, and gathered wild plant food. They practiced cremation and elaborate burial ceremonies. Occasionally, they sprinkled red ochre (powdered hematite) over the bodies of their dead and buried tools or weapons with them.

The Woodland cultures that followed these first primitive inhabitants introduced plant domestication. This gave them the leisure time to craft pottery, develop trade with their neighbors, and perfect the more sophisticated hunting method of the bow and arrow. The Iroquois culture evolved from these earlier Woodland cultures.

The lower Oswegatchie served as a boundary between the Mohawks and Oneidas, the easternmost tribes of the Iroquois nations. The Oswegatchie, Indian, and Black Rivers were an important transportation corridor leading to the heart of Mohawk country. The route is sometimes referred to as the Oswegatchie Trail. It was often used during beaver hunts and raids upon the Hurons in Canada. And it was probably used as well by a band of Mohawks sent by Sir William Johnson, a key figure in the French and Indian Wars, to burn Fort La Presentation at the present-day site of Ogdensburg. The fort was promptly rebuilt by its founder, Father François Picquet.

But the utilitarian hunting and fishing of the Woodland peoples left little indication of their passing. Indeed, there are few clues regarding any of this early human presence, though a handful of projectile points, dugout canoes, stone gouges, axe heads, pipes, and pestles have been uncovered. In the 1800s, well-known guide Alvah Dunning cut down a large cedar tree and discovered, under its roots, three earthen pots and a stone axe. Apart from such relics, however, there is little sign of the first Americans and no hard evidence at all of any permanent prehistoric settlements in the Adirondack region.

It is likely that French trappers of the early seventeenth century knew about the river. But the first white man to travel through the valley of the Oswegatchie and later write about it was probably a French Jesuit priest by the name of Joseph Antoine Poncet. His 1653 journey, as detailed in Hallie Bond's essay, became an ordeal of near heroic proportions. Father Poncet's report that the region through which they traveled had been hunted bare is further evidence that French trappers preceded him. Poncet was followed in turn by pioneer settlers, surveyors, sportsmen, loggers, and railroad men, each contributing to the ever-widening impact of humans upon the landscape.

The East or Main Branch of the Oswegatchie rises north of Partlow Milldam, where a number of small brooks that begin in

Herkimer County's Town of Webb come together in the remote forest known today as the Five Ponds Wilderness. From here, it is some twenty to thirty meandering and storied miles to the hamlet of Wanakena, where the river spills into Cranberry Lake.

There has long been a debate over the length of navigable waters on the East Branch. River distances are notoriously difficult to estimate, and the snake-like Oswegatchie is no exception. In the 1920s, prolific outdoor writer, T. Morris Longstreth, wrote that the river had "all the curves that Euclid knew and some that he dreamed about." The human history of the region is nearly as convoluted as the Oswegatchie itself.

Two of the earliest to stake a claim in this vast wilderness were Joseph Totten and Stephen Crossfield, who acquired more than a million acres south of Cranberry Lake from the Mohawks in 1771 for three cents an acre. (This was not quite the bargain it appeared, since King George III demanded various fees equivalent to many times the purchase price from the Mohawks before approving the sale.) Totten and Crossfield were shipwrights in New York who lent their names to this transaction for a consideration, which was to be one township divided between them. The real powers behind the great land deal were two brothers, Edward and Ebenezer Jessup, land speculators who were involved in many such transactions in northern New York. For their efforts, the Jessups have been largely ignored by history, while Totten and Crossfield gained a kind of immortality, their names forever emblazoned on Adirondack maps and in the deed transfers of every piece of property that they once nominally owned.

Between 1772 and 1800, several survey crews attempted to post the boundaries between this land and the vast, four-million-acre Alexander Macomb purchase. The result was a highly inaccurate map that Verplanck Colvin would work to correct a century later, as he and his men searched for the ancient blazes, struggling over nearly impassable terrain. In Colvin's *Topographical Survey of the Adirondack Wilderness for the year 1873*, he reported on the discovery of nearly twenty lost and unmapped ponds in this wilderness south of Cranberry Lake. On July 16, 1878, the Adirondack surveyor finally located the northwest corner of the Totten and Crossfield Purchase (the southern corner of St. Lawrence County). It was "the great pivotal point on which all the land titles of nearly five millions of acres depended," (*Seventh Annual Report of the Topographical Survey...to the year 1879*). He erected a stone marker on the spot. (See Nina H. Webb's essay, *Oswegatchie Odyssey*.)

As late as the 1850s, no roads at all reached the Cranberry Lake region. The closest a traveler could come was on three old "military" roads constructed about the time of the War of 1812. Though for years many people thought these crude paths were meant for moving troops, the roads were intended to open up the wilderness to prospective settlers. One such track ran from the Mohawk Valley to the St. Lawrence River via the central and western Adirondacks. It had actually begun as an Indian trail, and arrowheads have been found on this route a few miles above Inlet Flow.

By the early 1870s, travel had improved enough to allow novelist Irving Bacheller to journey south to Cranberry Lake by wagon from the family farm in Paradise Valley outside Canton. Bacheller and his boyhood friends were going "a-suckering" at the head of the lake where the run was on at the mouth of Sucker Brook. Rumbling along on what must have been an incredibly rough road, they passed the abandoned Iron Furnace at Clifton and, further on, the Great Windfall, where the cyclone of 1837 had left huge trees "broke and tumbled like ninepins." At Cranberry Lake, they boarded a little steamer that took them down to Sucker Brook. The suckers were "hard-meated" fish of six to ten inches in length. The boys had to lie face down on the rough boulders of the stingingly cold brook and grope for fish with their bare hands. In this manner, they could catch a hundred in a day, and the suckers, salted down in a big tub, would last all summer.

Bacheller later wrote about his guide, Philo Scott, one of the early settlers on the Oswegatchie, who also guided other men of letters, including Ernest Thompson Seton, Robert W. Chambers, and Booth Tarkington. Scott, sometimes called "Uncle Fide," was born in 1837 in the town of Brownville in Jefferson County, and from the age of seven, spent most of his life in the woods. By the time he was fifteen, hunting and trapping were his main business, and he often caught wolves and panthers in his traps. Scott was reputed to be the first settler of the wilderness south of Cranberry Lake and Dead Creek Flow.

Proof that Scott was indeed a St. Lawrence County (and probably Big Deer Pond district) resident by at least 1861 comes from his enlistment in Company D, 60th New York Volunteer Infantry on October 25th of that year. After service in the Civil War, Scott returned to Big Deer (which he called Lost Lake), constructed a shanty camp, and began catering to sportsmen who came over the old Albany Trail en route to Albany Lake, which Dr. W. Seward Webb later bought and called "Nehasane."

"Uncle Fide" was tall, strong, and lanky. According to contemporary observers, he had a generous degree of quaint Yankee humor and spoke with a drawl in the region's colorful vernacular. Naturally, some of his writer clients found him irresistible. Bacheller chronicled Scott's exploits and attempted to capture his figures of speech in his novel, *Silas Strong: Emperor of the Woods*, published in 1906.

In *Adirondack Pilgrimage*, Paul Jamieson describes Philo Scott as being nearly as celebrated a figure as Old Mountain Phelps, who also enjoyed the company of writers and artists, and who became something of a literary figure around Keene Valley. In the off-season, Scott and his wife lived in a cabin known as Scott's Bridge, near the hamlet of Oswegatchie. Every June, he would pack his provisions, his cow, and his decidedly unenthusiastic wife into his camp at Big Deer. He passed the summer there guiding and regaling sportsmen and novelists for a dollar a day for board and three more for a day's guiding.

Accounts of Scott's exploits were no doubt exaggerated over the years. It was said that he carried his new bride into camp in a rocking chair strapped to his back, some seven miles over a very rough trail (small wonder she was unenthusiastic). On another occasion, it was reported that he carried the carcass of a large deer, shot by one of his clients, over this same path from Dead Creek Flow to his camp, without once stopping. As the tales accumulated, some held that Scott's patrons killed so many deer over the years that a small island in the center of Lost Lake was covered with their bones.

In January 1905, Scott traveled with Bacheller and Tarkington to Saranac Lake's winter carnival. He then continued on to New York City, where he took a ride in the city's brand new subway. On his way home, the intrepid woodsman was said to have stopped off in Albany to lobby his old friend, James Whipple, the Forest, Fish and Game Commissioner, concerning the need for hunting and fishing licenses to stop the devastation of game. Whipple supposedly secured the privilege of the floor for Scott in the august chambers of the State Senate, and shortly thereafter New York decreed its first hunting and fishing license law, which included a stiff twenty-five dollar fine for non-resident hunters. A descendant of Scott's informs me, however, that despite exhaustive research, she has been unable to confirm that he ever addressed the Senate.

Philo Scott was not without competition on the Oswegatchie. At High Falls, another guide, Bert Dobson, conducted hunting camps for eighteen years at the turn of the century, also catering to many famous sportsmen. As many as forty guests at a time might come to Dobson's to watch three and four pound speckled trout attempt to leap the fifteen foot falls to spawn in the water upstream. None made it, however, and only puny trout were found above the falls. Dobson's business gradually fell apart after a disgruntled jobber chopped down the magnificent pines that grew nearby.

A pool below High Falls was dubbed "Carter's Magic Fish Box" by Cornelius Carter, another of the territory's early guides. In 1876, he lived a mile and a half away in the Plains, a clearing a mile long and half a mile wide situated between Roundtop and Threemile Mountains. No one knew the origins of this curious landscape, though the Plains was suspected to have been caused by a windfall or fire so many years in the past that the trees had long since decayed into the soil. When Dobson saw the area for the first time in 1897, he remarked, "Very little vegetation seemed to grow on this long stretch, but a more beautiful spot of nature I never had seen."

One feature of the Plains was the Boiling Spring, a pool of clear, cold water that rises up through the sand and never dries up, even in the most parched years. The place where the Plains met the Oswegatchie was called Carter's Landing. It was a long walk from where Carter launched his boat to his cabin, which was nestled against a huge wall of granite topped by white pines and balsams. At the edge of the meadows, there was said to be evidence of old stone ovens constructed during the War of 1812.

Cornelius Carter was the only permanent resident of the Plains for many years. A former schoolmaster and one-time deputy district attorney for St. Lawrence County, he had the misfortune of being suddenly struck deaf. Unable to practice his profession, he retreated to the solitude of the woods. He lived in the back country for twenty years, guiding and eventually publishing a book of verse with the help of his friend, L.C. Smith, the typewriter magnate.

One of the attractions near the headwaters of the Oswegatchie that helped keep guides like Carter and Dobson well employed was the great beaver dam. More than three hundred feet long and eight feet high, the structure created a pond for a huge colony of beaver. Fed by several cold streams, this pool grew so famous for its trout fishing in the 1800s that the designation, "Beaverdam," even appeared on commercial maps. As the nineteenth century ended, trappers all but wiped out the beaver, and this and other huge dams were ripped out to make way for a new type of adventurer, the outboard motor "sport."

It was through the efforts of one intrepid fisherman, deep in the trail-less backwoods, that a discovery even more surprising than the great beaver dam was made. The story is told by Peter V. O'Shea in his captivating book, *The Great South Woods: Rambles of an*

Adirondack Naturalist. Soon after World War II, an aircraft went down in a beaver meadow a short distance below Sliding Rock Falls on the Robinson River, a remote tributary of the Oswegatchie above High Falls. The site remained undiscovered for more than twenty years until it was found by the trout fisherman. Eventually, the plane's propellers were removed to a store owned by the local ranger, where they remained on display until they were stolen.

Hearty souls seem forever driven to the remotest parts of the river. Not far below the site of the great beaver dam was Pine Ridge, "by far the most breath-taking sight to be found in the Great North Woods," according to David F. Lane. Writing about the spot in *Adirondac* in 1949, he speaks of pines three to four feet in diameter and 150 feet tall, with the lowest branches 60 feet from the ground. Huge hemlocks and hard maples also abounded. Lane got there just in time, for many of the great trees he saw went down in the blowdown of 1950. But in silent screen days, such was the magnificence of Pine Ridge that it was chosen, Lane declares, as the location for James Fenimore Cooper's, *The Last of the Mohicans*.

There's little question that the primeval setting would have been picture perfect for such a film. Cooper himself couldn't have selected better, especially in light of the fact that, as Mohawk poet Maurice Kenny informs us, drawing-room novelist Cooper "could not have spotted an Indian in the forest if retaining his scalp depended on it." As it turns out, the Cooper story is probably apocryphal.

Paul Jamieson describes his efforts to verify Lane's romantic notion in his notes to Herbert Keith's book, *Man of the River*. Old timers had variously asserted that the film was about Cooper's Leatherstocking heroes, Natty Bumppo and Hawkeye, or possibly about Robin Hood, but the only 1920s films on these subjects made by American producers starred Wallace Beery (in both) and Douglas Fairbanks Sr. (in the latter). But there was no mention of such famous actors ever being in the North Country in the *Watertown Daily Times*, whose editor assured Jamieson that the presence of either would have caused a sensation. A more likely possibility, Jamieson speculates, is that the Pine Ridge "players" were involved in one of several educational films made by Yale University Press entitled *Chronicles of America*. One picture in this series was *Daniel Boone*, released in 1923. The area forest ranger circa 1960, Fred Griffin, said that when he first came on the job, he wondered about the remnants of platforms on Pine Ridge and was told that they had been left by a crew filming a western.

Actors and windstorms were not the only threats to the monarchs of Pine Ridge. By 1905, the Rich Lumber Company had constructed a logging railroad line that reached almost to High Falls, enabling access to the sixteen thousand acres south of Wanakena, the company town. In just seven years, this tract was stripped of its virgin spruce and pine. The river was sometimes choked with logs, much to the displeasure of the guides, whose business was gravely affected. Fortunately, lumbermen left some commercial grade timber standing along the river in support of the guides who operated sportsmen's camps.

Yet even these pines were in peril. In 1908, fires swept across tens of thousands of acres south and east of Cranberry Lake, burning the soil down to bedrock and at one point nearly surrounding little Wanakena. Townspeople dug deep holes to bury their valuables as the conflagration drew near. Eventually, the fires smoldered out once they reached virgin timber; dry slash left behind had fueled the blaze initially; thankfully, mature woods proved to be not so combustible.

Author Herbert Keith visited many of the old guides' camps as well as the Inlet House in 1907, when he traveled up the river with another well-known guide, Wilfred Morrison. Keith was only a boy at the time, but he soon came to realize that there was a tall tale associated with virtually every bend in the stream. Here was the battle ground where two guides settled a dispute armed with an axe and a double-barreled shotgun. There was Sugar Rapids where George Preston, after an eighteen-mile paddle, tipped over his canoe and lost a barrel of sugar within sight of his destination.

Farther along was the Old Root Hole, a huge pine bole embedded in sand. It washed out of the bank and floated down river, getting hung up in various places, finally reaching Inlet more than half a century after Keith first saw it. Then came the Seven Sisters Pines, which were seven large, dead pines when Keith saw them, all growing out of a single stump. Paddlers could see the pines approach and depart seven times as the river curled on its way. At Ross Rapids, Morrison and Keith heard the screech of the wheels of the Rich Lumber Company's Shay locomotive. They pulled ashore, walked up a narrow path and scrambled up the rail grade. Here, a crate fastened to a big tree had the words "Camp Betsy" written on it. This, Morrison told his astonished young companion, was his mailbox.

In his waning years, Morrison added to his considerable local reputation by saving the life of a man who had been shot in the leg while on a hunting trip above High Falls. The man's companions had run the six miles to Wanakena, where they learned that the nearest doctor was another nine miles beyond. The injured hunter would have to be taken out immediately by canoe, a paddle of twenty-one miles at night in a heavy rainstorm on a river that was rising rapidly. As the man's fate was discussed at Wanakena's general store, Morrison walked in, soaking wet and already tired from an eighteen mile hike. Hearing the story, he volunteered to walk into High Falls and bring the man out by canoe on this blackest of nights. And so he did, saving the man's life, though not his leg, which had to be amputated.

The first real sign of civilization—clean beds and indoor plumbing—as the river flowed north was the Inlet House, and the only way to get there was by an old wagon road from Star Lake or by trail along the river from Wanakena. The hotel, originally called Sternberg's, was built in the 1880s by George Sternberg, another guide drawn into the hospitality business. He was succeeded as proprietor by his son and eventually by Loring F. Moore, who bought the hotel in 1915.

Moore, David Lane wrote, was called the Paul Bunyan of the

Oswegatchie. A huge man with enormous hands and a grip of iron, he was reputed, at the age of 72, to have nearly broken the back of a husky, but drunk, young employee who attacked him. On the wall at Inlet House, Moore had hung an aging saber which he claimed had been unearthed along the old Albany Trail. Engraved on the weapon was the name of a British officer who fought in the American Revolution.

The buildings at Inlet were removed in the 1960s following the state purchase of the area. Now part of the Forest Preserve, the structures are gone and the site is marked by a parking lot and canoe launch. But Herbert Keith, while acknowledging that it was good for the river to be protected, harbored many fond memories of the days when a person could travel the Oswegatchie, stopping at the old guide camps and at Inlet House for a hot meal.

Today the East Branch from Inlet to Partlow Milldam, eighteen and-a-half miles, is protected and provides some of the best wilderness canoeing in the nation. And regardless of man's early intrusions, there are nearly fifty thousand acres along the East Branch that were never significantly burned or logged before the state acquired them as part of the W. Seward Webb purchase in 1896. This remains one of the largest tracts of virgin timber, of white pine, yellow birch, red spruce, and sugar maple, left in the Northeast, though much of the old growth went down in the storms of 1950 and 1995.

Despite the alteration of this great wilderness by logging, railroads, hurricanes and hotels, the Oswegatchie was still capable of attracting the interest of Robert Marshall, the original Adirondack Forty-Sixer and one of the founders of the Wilderness Society. Marshall hiked the area in the 1920s, visiting nearly a hundred ponds while conducting a national survey of forests that had not been seriously invaded by road or rail. In spite of this lingering remoteness, however, the moose, cougar, and wolf were already gone, hunted out half a century earlier by men who gave little thought to endangered species.

There were other signs that civilization was creeping into the backwoods. As early as 1879, Verplanck Colvin wrote: "The woods are thronged...hotels spring up as though by magic...and ladies clamber to the summits of those once untrodden peaks." For better or worse, people had begun to take notice of one of the last wild places in the eastern United States.

Isolation, thin soils, a harsh climate, and legions of mosquitoes and black flies cause some to view life in the Adirondacks, even today, as an exercise in endurance. But others have grown to love the untamed wildness of places like the upper Oswegatchie, for there is a magic about the Adirondacks, this land where men and women can roam and dream and still experience a primordial freedom. "Of what avail," Aldo Leopold once wrote, "are forty freedoms without a blank spot on the map?"

Barefoot in the Park

Gary Randorf

Over twenty years ago, while Clarence Petty and I were doing river surveys for the Adirondack Park Agency, we went along with authors Larry Pringle and Anne LaBastille to check out the Oswegatchie.

After camping along the river the first night, we headed toward Five Ponds the next morning. Though Clarence had seen this country before on numerous occasions, for the rest of us, I believe, it was a first visit. We were awed by the green lushness and in particular, by the stands of virgin hardwoods, and then by the huge pine and hemlock on the esker above the ponds. This whole territory smacked of primeval wonder.

I recall that Anne was hiking barefoot, an amazing feat to all who know the roughness of Adirondack trails. It reminded me of my college days when I had tough enough soles to Frisbee barefoot in wheat stubble!

Ultimately, we recommended to the New York Legislature that the Oswegatchie be added to the State Rivers System as a wild river, and it was. The effort was helped by a subsequent trip, in which we took State Senator Herb Posner into the same beautiful country, up that meandering slick of a river. Herb had never slept out before; his falling asleep while looking at the stars and experiencing the intense stillness just might have helped get the Rivers Bill through his Environmental Conservation Committee.

Pieces of the River

Mason Smith

How little we knew of the river; how little we sensed of its long running life and peregrinations. For us growing up in Gouverneur, I think it was only a great and dangerous alien thing dividing the town, felt more than seen, down below the level of our bicycles and sandlots, rolling brownly over a dam under the Main Street bridge and going on away somewhere still deeper down in its bracken-sided gully. We never went down those perilous jungled banks. I did not even cross that bridge on foot very often. I lived on the right, the good, the higher side of the river; the high school was three blocks from our house. So I speak under the penalty of privilege, and the West Side kids, who crossed the Oswegatchie on foot twice a day once they were out of grammar school, might tell a different story. I did think the West Side kids knew more than we, of what we shouldn't know; and knew it earlier, if you know what I mean. For, yes, the Oswegatchie was something like "the tracks" in Gouverneur.

In those early history lessons, we learned, from what I can remember, that Gouverneur Morris, whose brother Robert was "the financier of the revolution," owned a square old sandstone mansion out in Oxbow, to the northwest (and for all I know owned, also, a black woman whom I seem to see be-aproned in the doorway, in a picture of that house). But I don't recall that we learned anything at all about the river; hardly even that it made that oxbow, and many another, on its way to Ogdensburg. I don't think I picked up even that it did go to Ogdensburg—Ogdensburg was only where there was a bigger hospital, in which my older sister Sooki and I had our tonsils out. (Ether. Ice cream. Kindness.)

There was a power plant there by the bridge then, I think Oswegatchie Light and Power, where structural steel is stockpiled now. The river gave us our very illumination. But we didn't boat on it. I knew nobody who fished it. We swam, not in the scary, moving Oswegatchie, but in the scary, stagnant, bottomless marble pits, telling each other horrifying stories of un-recovered, drowned, white bodies glimpsed on dives into the lightless depths.

We crossed the river also on another older, narrower bridge, this one steel-trussed, silvery-painted (wooden-planked? maybe; clattery, I seem to recall), leading to the south, past the second-ranked of two movie theaters, and the bowling alley, and the dry cleaning place. Just beyond that bridge was the cemetery where one of my playmates' fathers worked—dug graves, we guessed, in the grass along a bend in that river, lending it still more spookiness. That's the bridge that goes toward the Country Club, toward Sylvia Lake, toward the mines with their red-tinged labor organizers. (Dad used to tell how his car was shadowed by an ominous black Chevrolet during one period when he was writing weekly editorials against a miner's strike.) It's the bridge where Dad always told us the story of the Indians and their runaway horse, and how the river came to be called *Hoss, We Gotchee!*

I don't know why he never told that story when we went over the Main Street Bridge, the Route 11 one. Maybe it was because when you crossed that smaller, clattery bridge, you were going toward the frontier, up-country, toward the mountains, or, rather, the woods; whereas when you crossed the Main Street bridge, you were just going to the West Side, or onward to another town east or west at the same altitude and level of civilization, more or less—

Antwerp, Philadelphia, Evans Mills, Watertown to the west, Canton and Potsdam to the east. Anyway, we got so we always sang the river's name as we crossed the backstreet bridge toward the rougher country, taking children's liberties with the pronunciation of *horse*, "Otchee-gotchee Riv-ver, Otchee-gotchee Riv-ver!"

What *did* they teach us in those schools? A little knowledge of the way the Oswegatchie ran would have done wonders to organize the world for a wondering child. It comes off the Adirondack plateau, yup, and goes to the St. Lawrence, yup; just that much would have been a help. But there are so many North Country rivers, one per town on Route 11, like grooves on a gravy-plate, and they go so deceivingly northwestward before entering it, that they fool you: Which one is which? Shouldn't this be the Grass, going in at Ogdensburg? It was heading this way. The Oswegatchie was heading for Alex Bay, or Heuvelton at least. But no, the Grass goes in past Waddington, and the Raquette past Massena.

Beside the bridge in Gouverneur, on the West Side of the river, north side of the street, close along the sidewalk, used to stand the Ruderman Machinery Exchange, with its metallic-painted, fake-stone block buildings with green trim. Inside were offices and dark rooms full of used electric motors and such, all blacks and grays. Down behind these buildings, spread out over a large area inside a bend of the river, was a lot of old machinery, large, hard shapes nondescript to me, but all somehow related to the mysterious business. Mr. Ruderman, dark-faced, dashing, partly disabled (he walked bent over, front and sideways, stiffly), rather threatening father of very inviting girls, made and lost larger amounts of money than we ever heard about otherwise (except in relation to Edward John Noble, the millionaire Gouverneur boy who owned ABC, I think-amazingly; he who got started making LifeSavers in a hotel room in Mexico, or some such story). Charlie Ruderman had an airplane with two motors; he often flew off in it to buy whole factories and paper mills, and take them apart and scatter the pieces along the bend of the Oswegatchie in his iron-oxide sculpture garden. He owned race-horses and a castle on an island in the St. Lawrence. He had famous fires. Once he told me (I was dating one of his daughters, carefully) that business was bad; he was depressed, so he'd bought himself a Packard 500 (black, lots of chrome) to cheer himself up and change his luck.

That area by the river where the dismembered factories once lay is all subsidized senior housing now. The tidy, uniformly inoffensive-colored, no-maintenance ghetto has made the river shore more decorous, I suppose. And it reflects, I suppose, an appreciation of the river as part of the scene, for a change.

That is a change. In all those Route 11 towns on all the North Country rivers from Watertown to Malone, the river used to be an uncelebrated back alley, given over to railroad tracks and industrial unsightliness. Even in early watermill days, the commercial buildings faced the horsey streets and bricked up their backs over the water, as if the all-important power and its source were merely useful and otherwise unmentionable; dangerous and probably unclean. Out-of-sight, out-of-mind: the rivers became a place for waste, the banks the least-valued land in town. An exception was the island in the Raquette at Potsdam, with its lovely trees and sandstone church and a view upstream that could not fail to be enjoyed. In the sixties, I took a boat out on the Raquette above that upstream view but still within the village limits and found it a sparkling sanctuary, wide and quiet, an archipelago of grass and willow islands, in clear, quick, shallow water over waving green weeds, full of bass and pike. We had beer-batter bass in a friend's backyard, with Ike and Tina Turner blasting from the porch, where faculty wives in shorts, with their shirt-tails tied over bare midriffs, danced as on a stage with intent to entertain. But looking for a home, I discovered that the poorest, cheapest housing was back along the river, in settings that only needed river-love to be quite beautiful.

With my indulgent mother in her sea-mist green Olds '88 convertible, I learned to drive on the humpy, molten, one-lane, paved roads that crossed and re-crossed the Oswegatchie north and west of Governeur. Scott Paper owned the mill at Natural Dam, I think; I still buy Scott from sentimental loyalty. I remember school field trips out there to the mill: the smell of the stew of cellulose in huge paddled vats, the web of paper being wrung dry of its Oswegatchie water between rollers in giant machinery rather like my father's newspaper press. The river made more than one mystifying reversal, out of sight behind the small meadows, granite pastures, and woodlands of the scrawny farms we drove by, homes and labor-sites of some of those "ain't-saying" schoolmates I didn't know so well, and popped up unexpectedly under another rusty steel skeleton with rattly planks, a sharp curve at the other end and perhaps a switch to gravel, which would raise the question, Where were we? Mom was a laissez-faire instructor and no navigator. I never really learned those roads; they and the river made a maze; I just learned to drive. We seldom could have told each other which side of the river we were on, but we came out somewhere recognizable, maybe west on 11, in Summerville or Evans Mills. Home, sweaty and dusty and sunburned, to take a bath in water that would look like weak coffee to me now; brown water, very brown in Gouverneur, seemed normal to me then.

We Smith kids spent half of every summer with our Everett grandparents at Lake Ozonia, near the Everett family farm at Fort Jackson, only returning for the week of the Gouverneur and St. Lawrence County Fair. The other half of the summer, we went off to a children's camp in the woods. The Ruderman girls went there too. And that's where, like the Rudermans, we made a start at being river-rats. Unlike most children's camps, Totem Camp wasn't on a lake, with a waterfront program involving war canoes and sailing boats; Totem Camp was on a forested stretch of the Oswegatchie, south of Harrisville.

Up there the river is quick-running and brown and rocky, and I think there were but two places on it fit for swimming. The safer one, still and shallow enough for the smaller kids, was called "The Bathtub." With almost no effort I can summon the amber gravel, the color and the feel of it in the drifting water, the slippery rocks, the paths along the shore. At the larger, deeper pool, there was a dock or float, with a diving board and room enough for what must have been pretty short swimming races, and I remember the spring-board on the dock, the hastily closed and opened jack-knives and hastily opened and closed swans, the cannonballs, and rather irregular frontwards and backwards flips. So much fun to do, all of these, that you swam breathless to the ladder, pulled up it faster than the water could run off your body, and sped dripping onto the rough-canvassed wooden board again, or stood shivering with impatience for your next turn, most kids breathing through their mouths, since their noses were pink-clipped.

That Oswegatchie water was truly brown. Even six inches of it in the bathtub at home had the color of weak coffee. I presume that Gouverneur village water is no clearer or bluer today. It was brown and soft and warm in the summer. Except for swimming in the river, and hiding along it during the days-long wars of capture-the-flag, we did not see it. We rode horses in the ring and on the meadows of the camp, did boondoggles in the crafts building, wrote post-cards home under orders in the dining room, entered the free-throw contest in the gym above the horse-stalls. I clearly remember Uncle Bill Graf teaching free-throw technique. He was the coach at Watertown High School, and you were supposed to practically do a deep knee bend with the ball between your legs and let out your breath and make a relaxed, hitch-free swing toward the rim while straightening your legs. Flaws of character revealed themselves as interference with this ideal, and I note that in these sad times nobody even aspires to it.

This was war-time. I was seven, eight, nine. I was so homesick once my first year that Aunt Helen took me with her on some errand to Harrisville in the station wagon. A partridge strayed into the twisting gravel road and Aunt Helen did her best to hit it, without running flat over it. She missed it, despite an alarming zig-zag and slide, but I was much impressed. She would have pulled the guts out of it with her bare fingers and tossed it in back for supper, she said.

Dad was in the South Pacific, and I remember the excitement of a false Armistice, when a siren summoned us all to council in the middle of the day and we were told the war was over. It wasn't. But Mary Jane Ruderman recently showed me a photograph of all us campers surrounding Uncle Bill, in the ceremonial circle near the horse-barn/gym, where we were celebrating the real Armistice, the real end of the war. A banner stretches around the outskirts of the pow-wow which says, "WE GAVE THE JAPS ATOMIC ACHE."

Once in the eighties, Hallie and I made an overnight canoe trip up the Oswegatchie above Inlet. We started late in the afternoon, after attending a wedding in the countryside near Canton. At the put-in we met a young German couple with a baby, just getting off the river from a long trip all the way from the Bog River, involving the four mile carry from Low's Lake to the upper East Branch, in the very peak mosquito season. They weren't communicative. I think they wanted their money back, and possibly their vows. Otherwise, I chiefly remember what fun it was for us, getting our fairly newly-wed teamwork going, bending our eighteen and-a-half-foot E. M. White guide model wood and canvas canoe around the corners. We paddled until twilight, cooked a steak, and disposed of a bottle of wine, and next morning paddled on, as far as we could go and still get out in daylight, expert wrappers by that time and lustful for river-corners ever since.

You might say we became river-lovers *sans frontiéres*. I would have said that we were a sadly un-watery society in the North Country, despite our wealth of rivers, but perhaps it is not so. Perhaps the growing up in Gouverneur on the Oswegatchie put rivers in our blood, in spite of us, and made river-rats of us, in spite of our early fear and ignorance. Something did it, to some of us—my brother Everett, for instance. He and I christened the first Rushton-type, cedar-lapstrake boat we built, in 1973, with a run down the St. Regis from Paul Smiths to Santa Clara, an unforgettable trip. With an innocent apostasy to the Oswegatchie, we called the St. Regis "our maternal river," because it picks up at the outlet of Lake Ozonia, which we think of as our family's spiritual home. Since then, with his brother-in-law, Everett has built a hydroelectric plant on that stream, in St. Regis Falls. He's also become a St. Lawrence River-rat of sorts, working as curator and consultant at the Antique Boat Museum in Clayton. I myself de-fluvenated to the Big River too, working as a purser on tour-boats my first summer out of high school, and later living on a Canadian island in our grandfather's first-war Army tent and getting my groceries by sailing-canoe, while making my first attempt at writing. And to the Rudermans, too, especially Mary Jane—talk of river-rats! Mary Jane ended up with one of her father's defunct paper mills, on the Black River in Carthage, and with tremendous vision and tenacity, redeveloped its water-power possibilities—another nail in Niagara-Mohawk's coffin. (And note the rivers in that name, if there's any doubt how rivers get into everybody's veins and circuitry.)

Hallie and I and water-babies Alex and Maggie now live on the shore of a wide part of the Raquette in Long Lake, and from this point we play, as we can and as we are moved, in the Grass, the St. Regis, the Bog, the Hudson, the Ausable, etc.—rivers in all directions, with no favorites. It all goes by rivers, in the end, and a child of one river is a child of all.

Sometimes now I think of these towns, this civilization on the rivers of the North Country, as the very saddest things. I know the people are not sad; they live good lives; the people are fine; yada, yada, yada. But please look at the state of things physical. A culture developed here in the nineteenth century that was beautiful in its material being, as long as it was growing, improving, and was only what it was of its own nature. There were lumbering, mining, agriculture, water-power towns, and buildings and other modifications to the landscape that comported with these things. But all or almost all of the buildings made in that long, slow expansion were necessarily temporary: wooden. And yet they have lasted beyond their need and relevance until most are shambles now, though still used (very differently used). Meanwhile, new, temporary and cheap styles of buildings have been built, various cycles and fashions of these, without regard for cultural harmony with the old. A beautiful nineteenth century house decays, a trailer or a ranch or a modular is used and decays beside it, thanks to the economic struggles of the North, thanks to the decline of maintenance discipline which somehow got disconnected from the discipline of want. A totally disordered architecture results. The decline of agriculture, the power-lines, and the spread of irrelevant business and irrelevant country living along the roads, have practically destroyed the physical beauty of the countryside. And then, as if to put an exclamation point to man-made ruin, there was the ice storm of 1998, snapping off the top of every tree and making the pathetic works of man more nakedly obvious.

What to do for the pitiful region, I sometimes wonder; what is to be done? I think nothing. The hateful, horrid, sacred *Economy* rules, as if breathing humans have no choice. But whatever it is that will be done, it starts with the rivers. This is still a young civilization, as desperate and pragmatic as Alaska's. We humans and our works on the face of the North Country need to get much older, until all of our works are four or five hundred years old, as honored as the lands and waters are. We're at least beginning to honor the waters.

Highlander

Christopher Angus

It has always been here, or so it seems: constant, steadfast, durable...immutable. With a sense of proprietorship, the tree surveys the Oswegatchie highlands. This entails more than simply scanning the long, open stretch of river or out across the esker and the surrounding wetlands. The great white pine feels rather than sees its place in the scheme of things.

It feels the moisture content of the air, the tightness of dry soil compacting fine roots, the warm glow of sunlight beating down in full midsummer glory. It feels the paws and claws of squirrels, chipmunks, raccoons, porcupines. It feels the tension in one high limb as an osprey crouches, then springs to the chase.

The tree feels, too, the strange internal fire of life, of sap flowing, of the testing and drilling and hollowing of ants, termites, and salamanders nestled under its protective bark. It feels the sharp thrum of the pileated woodpecker's beak as it seeks out this living nourishment. And deep in its bark, it feels the lacerations of the black bear as bruin marks his own territory.

Each thing the tree feels triggers a memory, for within its fibers resides much of the history of this place. For two hundred years the tree has been in this spot, probing, testing, absorbing the lifeblood of the esker, embracing the highlands. Two hundred years have passed since the tree's spirit first resided in a bristled cone high atop its forebear. Jarred loose by a fierce winter gale, it tumbled to the snow-covered forest floor. There it lay, slowly disintegrating into the rich soil until finally, after one heavy July rain, life stirred.

In the early years, the young pine grew slowly under the wing of its patriarch, protected from ice and wind. A silent understudy, it fought for its own small niche of the highlands. Sheltered beneath those immense spreading branches, the tree sank its deep taproot, fighting to establish itself quickly, as all things must in the forest.

Then, one warm spring afternoon, just as the sap of life began to stir, its protector was gone in an instant. Two small creatures had come along the esker and, in less than an hour, pushed hard, shiny edges of steel through the thick-grained, living tissue, cutting off the rising sap and sending the huge tree thundering to the forest floor with a roar that echoed across the hills and shook its scion to its own small roots.

For many years, the young tree felt an emptiness, almost a sense of imbalance, as the very soil struggled to recover from the loss of so many thousands of anchoring root stems. For a score of years, it was touch and go for the small pine. An ice storm bent and split many branches, blight browned its needles one dry summer, it developed a permanent lean away from the belligerent north wind. Yet it struggled on, soaring higher, roots thrusting ever lower, seeking nourishment even from the decaying limbs of its destroyed parent.

Though it labored in the absence of its forebear, the young tree also benefited from that absence. Now the sun's rays struck directly, infusing the tree with life-giving warmth and sustenance. Now its own roots were the main path for the nutrients and moisture so desperately needed during the dry months. And as the young tendrils grew, so they spread, probing each new avenue, each weakening of the soil and worm tunnel, burrowing, seeking, at last coming into contact with smooth, Precambrian granite.

Undaunted, the roots advanced across the top of the rock and down its sides, searching like nomads in a desert, encircling, grasping for every indentation and crack. Searching for weakness, for moisture. Holding. Anchoring to the nurturing earth.

This new summer has been dry, and the tree is aware of a tightness in its roots, a stiffening in its branches, of a decline in its ability to bend before the blast. The esker itself has dried to near powdery fineness. The soft, deep bed of needles that covers the hill is centuries old, decaying by degrees to a rich, red soil. But now, on the surface, the needles are tinder dry and the risk of fire is real. The tree senses this danger, but can only stretch its limbs to the sky...and wait.

As it waits, it remembers. It remembers other droughts, some hundreds of years in the past. In the tree's hard core resides the memory of the barren early years when a great dryness slowed its growth. That memory is like the ache of a long-endured rheumatism. The tree's memories do not reside in a single place but spread throughout from topmost branch to lowest root. The tree remembers with a shudder of hard tissue, with the vibration of sap flowing in long, vein-like corridors. And...it enjoys its memories.

The tree remembers a band of Indian hunters that once camped and fished beneath it. It can still recall the feel of branches springing under the bare feet of one small Indian boy. Climbing to the very top in a windstorm, he clung for hours, exhilarating in the elements and in his own place in the order of things. The boy was the only human to ever climb the tree.

The tree remembers when it once belonged to a larger grove of giants, all proudly waving their wide boughs before the incessant winds that bathed the top of the esker. It is a painful memory, for most of its fellows are gone now. How strange it had been...those distant sounds growing louder day by day, like an approaching swarm of bees, until the noise became continuous, almost unbearable, and accompanied by the crash of comrades toppling to the forest floor. Closer and closer the sounds came until the tree could see its friends, even its own children, surrendering before the diminutive creatures that moved along the esker. Then, just as resignation set in, the creatures disappeared, and the tree found that it was no longer part of a vast community of its fellows. Now, only a few of the big trees remained, towering over the hardwoods, the maple, oak, and birch, towering over the spruce and larch, the low-lying cedar and alder.

For the hundredth time this day, the tree sniffs the sky, expanding its pores. There is something there...a distant increase in humidity, too slight for any but the most water-starved tissue to detect. The tree returns to its thoughts.

Deep in the pine's side lies an intruder. Cold and hard, it does not belong. It is a bullet, shot by an early homesteader hoping to feed his family. The shot missed its target and lodged forever in the heavy bark. The tree remembers how the deer lowered its antlered head just as the bullet was launched with a clap of thunder, and how the projectile passed harmlessly above it. The tree was content that it took the bullet for the deer.

Again. Yes. There *is* moisture in the air. Sky-hugging needles know at once that a change in the weather has been heralded. It will take time for that awareness to penetrate to every part of the massive sentinel. But in a very real way, the tree as a whole already feels relief. A storm is coming!

Throughout the long afternoon, the front saunters in. Hot rays of sunlight are obliterated as a fresh wind gathers the clouds and whips the tree's branches. A sigh of anticipation sweeps across the esker as the forest prepares for its long-promised renewal. By nightfall, the wind has grown stronger and a fierce onslaught now appears to be just over the horizon. Sensing the low rumble of distant thunder, the tree shudders, for it was once witness to the lightning strike that destroyed a comrade nearby.

With complete darkness come sudden streaks of lightning, revealing, in frozen instants of time, a world vastly different from that peaceful summer morning now so far away. The tree and its fellows begin to prepare. The wet still to come will be welcome, but the rising wind demands attention to the details of survival. Fibers of branch and bark and core stretch, lengthening the filaments of lignin that will allow the tree to exceed its normal reach. Roots tighten, fighting for every molecule of hold upon the granite. Pine needles retract, gripping their stems snugly.

Now the wind reaches gale force and the first large drops spatter against the bark. The tree's branches fly wildly, seemingly possessed by some demon they will go through any contortion to exorcize. An eagle's nest, snugly fastened in a high notch of branches, comes apart and blows away, forcing two young eaglets to learn to fly at once under the worst of conditions, or perish.

Midst the roar of thunder, the tree detects a crashing of another kind as other forest giants lose the battle and topple. Its own fibers stretch to their limit, yet still the wind increases. Limbs extend until they can extend no farther, and the tree fights to resist a cataclysmic crack deep within. Along the length of the esker, stout comrades succumb, falling away on all sides, tearing up massive earthen-work holes in the duff, suddenly exposing small ground dwellers to the ferocity of the storm.

Now the tree fights for its life. Now it understands that this is a storm unlike any it has known in its two hundred years. The wind shrieks its demonic fury like a million ghosts fleeing through the sky. A large limb snaps, breaks off like a blade of grass, and vanishes into the darkness. The monarch leans one way and then the other, bending farther than it has ever bent before. A neighbor falls and brushes the tree, snapping a dozen more branches. The pine shudders through its entire length, even as it makes one final attempt to tighten its hold upon the rock beneath.

Then...pain. Separation. Roots tearing, popping. Memories flood down splintering sap trails. Youth, bear, Indian boy, summer dry, winter cold, ice splitting branch, loon, beavertail, storm, rain, wind, darkness...the rushing earth.

Contributor Biographies

Christopher Angus's articles and essays on the Adirondack region have appeared in many publications, including the *New York Times*, *Albany Times-Union*, *Adirondack Life*, *Canoe*, *American Forests*, *Adirondac*, and *The Adirondack Explorer*. His work also appears in a number of anthologies, including *Living North Country*, *Rooted in Rock*, and *The Adirondack Reader*. For many years a weekly outdoor columnist for the *St. Lawrence Plaindealer* and the *Advance News*, he also served as Book Review Editor for *Adirondac Magazine* for ten years. He is the author of *Reflections From Canoe Country—Paddling the Waters of the Adirondacks and Canada*, *Images of America: St. Lawrence County* (with Susan Wood), and *The Extraordinary Adirondack Journey of Clarence Petty: Wilderness Guide, Pilot and Conservationist*. He has been active in lobbying for the Environmental Protection Act and in efforts to reopen Adirondack rivers to the public.

Hallie Bond is a curator at the Adirondack Museum in Blue Mountain Lake where, in 1991, she completely revised the boat exhibit. Out of that work came *Boats and Boating in the Adirondacks*, an illustrated history and catalog of the museum's collection. Bond has a bachelor's degree in history from the University of Colorado, an M.A.

in Medieval Studies from the University of York (U.K.), and an M.A. in American History with a Certificate in Museum Studies, which she earned as a Hagley Fellow at the University of Delaware.

She was the curator of a temporary exhibit on summer camps in the Adirondacks and is the editor and a contributor to the resulting publication, *A Paradise for Boys and Girls: Children's Camps in the Adirondacks*. She teaches a course in Adirondack cultural history for the St. Lawrence University Adirondack semester. Hallie Bond lives in Long Lake with her husband, fellow contributor Mason Smith, and their two children.

Charles Brumley has been a resident of Saranac Lake since 1984 and has summered at Piseco Lake for over forty years. A former licensed guide, he is the author of *Guides of the Adirondacks: A History*; *Ripples From the Paddle: Adirondack Stories*; *Cry Me Home, Loon*; and, with photographer Carl Heilman, *Wild New York*. He has also written for regional publications such as *Adirondack Life*, *Barkeater*, and *The Franklin County Historical Review*.

He and his wife, Karen Loffler, perform in the folk music duo "Wood-heat."

Neal Burdick, a Plattsburgh native and Phi Beta Kappa graduate of St. Lawrence University, holds a Ph.D. in American Studies. He is publications writer/editor and an advanced writing instructor at St. Lawrence, and a freelance editor and writer. He has published in genres from poetry to book reviews and essays, and in publications from Fodor's travel books to *Blueline*. He is Editor-in-Chief of *Adirondac*, the magazine of the Adirondack Mountain Club, and of the club's series of hiking guides, and a frequent contributor to *Adirondack Explorer* and *Adirondack Life*. Co-editor of the anthology *Living North Country* and of a forthcoming new edition of *The Adirondack Reader*, he has edited numerous book manuscripts about the Adirondacks for regional publishing houses. He has been a panelist for New York Foundation for the Arts and Adirondack Center for

Writing (ACW) writing contests and a commentator on North Country Public Radio. He is on the Steering Committee of the ACW and is a co-director of St. Lawrence's Young Writer's Conference.

Paul Jamieson, Professor Emeritus of English at St. Lawrence University, is the doyen of Adirondack writers. He is the author of the classic and much-copied guidebook, *Adirondack Canoe Waters: North Flow*, and the editor of *The Adirondack Reader*, an invaluable source-book of writings on the region. His other books include *Adirondack Pilgrimage* and *Uneven Ground*. For more than a quarter of a century, he led the battle to reopen Adirondack rivers to recreational paddling—a battle that has, for all intents and purposes, been won as a result of recent court opinions.

Christine Jerome lives in western Massachusetts. A former managing editor of *Car and Driver* and *New England Monthly* magazines, she now freelances as an editor and writer. She is the author of *An Adirondack Passage: The Cruise of the Sairy Gamp*, and is working on *The Nessmuk Reader*, a collection of travel writing by George Washington Sears.

Maurice Kenny, born in Watertown, New York, in 1929, is one of the most celebrated Native American poets of all time. He has published over thirty books of poetry, fiction, and essays. His *Mama Poems*, an extended elegy, won the American Book Award in 1984, and his books *Blackrobe*, *Isaac Jogues*, and *Between Two Rivers* were nominated for the Pulitzer Prize. Kenny considers his most important work to be *Tekonwatonti, Molly Brant, 1735-1795*, a historical poetry journey in many voices that honors the Mohawk figure Molly Brant and explores an important time in American history when the British, French, Iroquois, and colonists were engaged in a monumental collision of cultures. Calling Kenny "a master lyricist," Joseph Bruchac writes: "Kenny is the creator of a new form of dramatic monologue in his recreations of the voices and time of Isaac Jogues and Molly

Brant." For the past four years, between New York and Mexico, Kenny has extended his method of historic poetry in writing a new book, *Conversations with Frida Kahlo: Collage of Memory*.

Kenny has taught in many places, including St. Lawrence University, Paul Smith's College, the University of Victoria, Lehigh University, and the University of Oklahoma. In 1995, St. Lawrence University awarded Kenny with the degree of Doctor of Literature. He currently teaches at the State University of New York at Potsdam as "writer in residence." His latest poetry collection is *Carving Hawk: New and Selected Poems*.

Michael Kudish, retired Professor in the Division of Forestry at Paul Smith's College, now lives in the Catskills, where he continues a fascination with railroads that began with his books *Where Did the Tracks Go* and *Railroads of the Adirondacks—A History*. He recently published *Where Did the Tracks Go in the Western Adirondacks?*, the first in a four volume set entitled *Mountain Railroads of New York State*. He is also the author of *The Catskill Forest: A History* and three books on the vegetation of the Adirondacks, including *Adirondack Upland Flora*.

Donald Morris was born and raised in Miami, Florida, moved to Nashville, Tennessee, then settled in the North Country—first in Canton and then in Saranac Lake—where he currently resides. Don figures that, at this rate, he will eventually be living near the Arctic Circle. He lives with his beautiful wife, Karen, and his two wonderful kids, Chris and Katelynn. He is a psychologist employed by New York State, with expertise in forensic evaluations and setting up specialized treatment programs. Don loves the Adirondacks and spends much time hiking, skiing, and paddling in some of the most beautiful areas in the Park—the Oswegatchie basin being among his favorites. He is co-author (with Paul Jamieson) of *Adirondack Canoe Waters: North Flow*. He has written for *Adirondack Life* and *Adirondac* magazines and has also published a number of research articles in the field of psychology.

Clarence Petty is a second generation Adirondack guide who led many hunting and fishing expeditions in the early part of the twentieth century. He has been a member of the Civilian Conservation Corps (CCC), a forest ranger, and a pilot, with seventy years of experience inside the Adirondack Park mapping the wilderness, fighting forest fires, and serving as Governor Averell Harriman's personal pilot. A member of Governor Rockefeller's 1968 Study Commission on the Future of the Adirondacks and of the APA during the period of its turbulent formation, he is a longtime chronicler of and advocate for wilderness preservation in the Adirondacks. Widely recognized as the most knowledgeable person alive on the Adirondack region, he is the recipient of numerous awards, including the prestigious Bob Marshall Award from the Wilderness Society. *The Extraordinary Adirondack Journey of Clarence Petty: Wilderness Guide, Pilot and Conservationist*, by Christopher Angus, is the story of his life.

Gary Randorf is a well-known photographer and writer who became the Adirondack Park Agency's first park naturalist. He spent ten years as Director of the Adirondack Council and then returned to the APA to help with the opening of the new Adirondack Park Visitor Interpretive Centers. He is the author of *The Adirondacks: Wild Island of Hope.*

Mason Smith grew up in Gouverneur, the son of the local newspaperman. His two three-act plays about the North Country during the Seaway construction years, *Forces* and *The 'lunge Campaign*, were produced at SUNY Potsdam in the '60s. His first novel was *Everybody Knows and Nobody Cares.* In the '70s and '80s, he contributed frequently to *Sports Illustrated*, *Adirondack Life*, *Gray's Sporting Journal* and other magazines. His most recent novel is *Florida*, the tragic yet humorous story of a winter's startling events in a small North Country town.

He is now at work on another three-act play called *Hospice Shmospice!*

about an old man who decides to sail away across the Atlantic instead of hooking up the oxygen and waiting it out. Mason lives in Long Lake and is an accomplished boat builder and restorer.

Dick and Barbara Tiel live in Canton, New York and are long-time Adirondack paddling enthusiasts. On July 15, 1995, they were among a number of campers caught in the great microburst windstorm that swept across the Five Ponds Wilderness causing widespread devastation.

Nina H. Webb, Adirondack 46er and fourth generation summer resident of the northern Adirondacks, was long active in groups committed to the preservation of the Adirondacks, including the Adirondack Trail Improvement Society, the Adirondack Mountain Club, the Adirondack Chapter of the Nature Conservancy, the Association for the Protection of the Adirondacks, Adirondack Discovery, and Friends of the Adirondack Museum. After extensive research into the life and accomplishments of Verplanck Colvin, she constructed and launched a replica of Colvin's patented portable boat, the Ampersand. She authored a popular biography about Colvin entitled, *Footsteps Through the Adirondacks*, and lectured widely on the subject of Verplanck Colvin.